ONOMATO PERA-PERA

An Illustrated Guide to Japanese Onomatopoeia

オノマトペラペラ

マンガで日本語の擬音語・擬態語

The Japan News
読売新聞英字新聞部 監修

MIZUNO Ryotaro
水野良太郎 編

東京堂出版

はじめに

　これは漫画家の仕事だ！──本書は日本語の擬音語・擬態語（onomatopoeia）について，その特異な魅力を漫画のシチュエーションで紹介した書籍である。日本人なら大抵の人が日常，口にし，耳にし，使い分けている日常語ではあるが，不思議なことに言語として省みられることは少ないように思われる。大衆演芸の舞台や落語に登場する人のよい庶民や，昨今では映画やテレビ，ラジオ・ドラマなどのラフな日常会話で使われたり，作られたりする。印刷媒体では漫画のセリフやギャグの一部として比較的使用頻度が高いように思われるが，あまり気に留められることもなく，コミュニケーションの道具として軽く考えられることが多い。しかし私は，人々の暮らしや歴史，文化の発展に最も深く付き合ってきた言葉の化石のような存在ではないかと考えてきた。

　宮沢賢治の『風の又三郎』の描写にはこのうえない迫力を感じ，春の海を「のたり のたり」と謳いあげた与謝蕪村にいたっては，その表現の豊かさに息をのんだ。何もない静寂な空間にわざわざ「シーン」という文字が書き込まれるとき，これは「音」なのか「情景」の一部なのか，日本人は考えもせずに次の場面に視線を移すだろう。だが外国人はそうは行かない。「何だ，これは？」と悩んでしまうのだ。

　私の職業は漫画家で，物語性のある作品では擬音語・擬態語を効果的に使う世界で仕事をしてきた。実際のところ，漫画の魅力のひとつは，擬音語・擬態語を如何に巧く取り込むかで勝負するところにある。

　私が擬音語・擬態語を特別に意識し始めたのは，日本語を学ぶ外国の友人たちが戸惑い，苦労していたからだ。漢字はさほど難しいとは思わないという。だが，数詞と敬語，そして擬音語・擬態語の使い分けには頭を抱え，その難しさに苦笑するのであった。そこで，私は一肌脱ごうと思いたった。漫画家がいちばん付き合ってきたジャンルではないか。

　過去に類似の書籍もあったが，擬音語・擬態語がもっとも有効に魅力を発揮するのは，実践的な環境説明にあり，情景の説明に使われる場合は感性の

遊び心が不可欠になる。しかも，日本は世界でも稀な擬音語・擬態語の大国であり，独自の歴史と伝統を引き継いだ固有の文化と習慣が関わってくるため，外国語に翻訳したり説明したりするのは一筋縄ではいかない。

とりわけ本書が類書を寄せ付けないのは，擬音語・擬態語を漫画表現の中に据え置いたことと，英語と日本語のすぐれたバイリンガル・スピーカー諸氏の参加である。それも新聞報道のベテラン記者諸氏で，英語と日本語での表現力においてはプロ中のプロである。私は日頃から「翻訳」という作業は異文化間の交流であり，橋渡しだと確信してきた。それだけに複眼的で広い視点と豊かな言語感性がなければ勤まらないと考えていたので，彼らに出会えたのは大きな感動になった。

本書は，読売新聞の発行する英字新聞「The Daily Yomiuri（デイリー・ヨミウリ）」に1996年より掲載している「ONOMATO-PERA-PERA」を，1996年から2010年までの掲載分から抜粋し，東京堂出版が編集し直したものである。なお，デイリー・ヨミウリは2013年4月に「The Japan News（ジャパン・ニュース）」に名称変更した。

「ONOMATO-PERA-PERA」の新聞連載にあたっては，原案と漫画を水野良太郎が担当し，読売新聞英字新聞部が英訳を行った。今回の書籍化にあたり，連載時の原稿から新たに日本語説明文の作成と英文のチェック・修正を読売新聞英字新聞部のスタッフが行い，全面的な見直しによって，より完成度の高い内容に仕上げた。読者はThe Japan Newsのスタッフの情熱と心意気にも触れていただきたい。

日本語の解説に目を通すと，日本語と英語の違いや，感性の違い，文化の違いも浮きあがってくる。この本を手に取ったことをきっかけに，より多くの読者が日英の擬音語・擬態語の表現に関心を寄せられることを願っている。

また，きわめて面倒な原稿整理と分類などの編集作業を一人でがんばって下さった東京堂出版編集部・酒井香奈氏に「編集者魂」を見た思いがする。合わせて厚くお礼を申し上げたい。

2014年6月

水野良太郎

PREFACE

This is work of manga artists! This book describes the fascination of Japanese onomatopoeias in manga scenes. Japanese people often hear and use onomatopoeias in everyday life, but they seldom reflect on them as language. The onomatopoeias are used and made by characters representing common people in popular plays or rakugo; in colloquial conversation in movies and radio dramas, and on TV. In printed media, they seem to be often used in manga, but they are rarely paid attention to and are lightly regarded as a simple communication tool. However, I think they are like "language fossils" which are connected deeply to our life, history and culture.

I was impressed with the expressions in "Kaze-no-matasaburo" by Miyazawa Kenji. I was very moved to read Yosa Buson writing of the spring sea as "notari notari".

In quiet, empty manga scenes, "Shiin" often appears. What does "Shiin" mean? Is it a sound or part of the background? We Japanese don't care at all, but foreign people probably wonder about it.

I have worked for a long time in manga art where onomatopoeias are used effectively. In fact, one of manga's fascinations is the way artists put a lot of effort into using onomatopoeias effectively.

When I saw my foreign friends were puzzled and confused by them, I began to pay particular attention to them. They said the kanji characters weren't very difficult, but proper use of Japanese numerals, honorifics and onomatopoeias were very annoying to them. They said this and gave wry smiles. I thought I wanted to help them, because I was an expert at onomatopoeias.

In the past, there were similar books about Japanese onomatopoeias, but they couldn't translate them clearly to foreign languages. They are used as effective explanations of the circumstances and express playful feelings as well. In addition, there are a lot of onomatopoeias which are associated with culture and customs peculiar to Japanese history and traditions. It is not easy to translate or explain Japanese onomatopoeia.

The features of this book that are superior to others are placing onomatopoeias in manga scenes, and the participation of excellent bilingual speakers of Japanese and English who are experienced newspaper reporters and have professional skills communicating in Japanese and English. I have always thought translation is an important task for intercultural exchange and mediation. Therefore, as I have thought it requires a broad view and rich linguistic sensibility, I was very glad to have worked with them.

This book was produced by editing the extracts of the articles "ONOMATO-PERA-PERA" run in The Daily Yomiuri published by The Yomiuri Shimbun from 1996 to 2010. (The name "The Daily Yomiuri" was changed to "The Japan News" in April, 2013.)

In running the articles "ONOMATO-PERA-PERA", Mizuno Ryotaro was in charge of the original plans and making the manga, and the staff of The Yomiuri Shimbun were in charge of English translation. In editing those articles into this book, the staff of The Yomiuri Shimbun added Japanese explanations, checked English sentences and rewrote them. Reviewing them completely made this book very mature. I would like you to feel the passion and spirit of the staff.

After reading this book, you can see the difference between Japanese and English, in sensibility and in culture. I hope a lot of readers will become more interested in Japanese and English onomatopoeias because of this book.

And last but not least, I very much thank Ms. Sakai Kana at the editorial department of Tokyodo-shuppan, who did the troublesome editing work on this book by herself. I am sure that she is a true editor.

June, 2014
MIZUNO Ryotaro

もくじ Contents

はじめに *Preface* ... 1

Chapter 1 さまざまな様子 — *Various Situations* ... 7
Chapter 2 いろいろな動き — *Various Movements* ... 31
Chapter 3 料理・食べもの — *Cooking & Food* ... 53
Chapter 4 気持ち・感情 — *Feelings & Emotions* ... 79
Chapter 5 体調・健康 — *Conditions & Health* ... 101
Chapter 6 ファッション・身だしなみ — *Fashion & Appearance* ... 115
Chapter 7 仕事・オフィス — *Work & Office* ... 131
Chapter 8 天気・気候 — *Weather & Climate* ... 149
Chapter 9 季節・自然 — *Seasons & Nature* ... 167

索引 *Index* ... 180

- 本書は，デイリー・ヨミウリ（現ジャパン・ニュース）に1996年から2010年まで連載された記事を再編集し，9つのテーマに分けて収録しています。
- 各ページには，マンガとその英訳，そのページのマンガで取り上げたオノマトペの解説を掲載しています。
- 書籍化にあたり，解説は日本語と英語を併記しました。
- オノマトペには複数の意味を持つものもあります。本書では，それぞれのマンガのシチュエーションに沿って解説を付しています。

- This book was made by re-editing articles from 1996 to 2010 from The Daily Yomiuri (present name, The Japan News) and categorizing them into nine themes.
- The manga, its English translation and the explanation of its onomatopoeias are shown on each page.
- This book has Japanese explanations of the onomatopoeias and English translations printed next to each other.
- Some onomatopoeias have plural meanings. Therefore, their explanations are shown according to the situations of the manga in this book.

Chapter 1

Various Situations
さまざまな様子

Various Situations

ゴロゴロ

① *goro goro* / *pikat*
② — *Onaka ga suite **guu guu** ....* (I'm hungry and my stomach is growling.)
　— *Onaka no choshi ga warukute **goro goro** ...!* (Something is causing my stomach to make a noise.)
③ *goron* / *pata pata*
　— *Atsui toki wa nani mo sezu, heya de **goro goro** ...* (When it's hot, I just lie down in my room and do nothing.)
④ *nyaao* / *goro goro*
　— *Nodo o narashite amaeteru no ne ...* (You are fawning on me by purring.)

ゴロゴロ(①) [*goro goro*]：雷の鳴る音。
The sound of thunder.

ピカッ [*pikat*]：何かが光る様子。
Describes something flashing.

グウグウ [*guu guu*]：腹の鳴る音。特に腹が空いている時の音。
The sound the stomach makes, particularly when a person is hungry.

ゴロゴロ(②) [*goro goro*]：腹の調子が悪い時に腹が鳴る音。
The sound made when one's stomach is queasy.

ゴロン [*goron*] / **ゴロゴロ(③)** [*goro goro*]：物が転がる音。または，人がくつろいで寝転がる様子。「ゴロゴロする」は，特に何をするでもなく時を過ごす様子。
When something rolls down or a person lies down, relaxing his or her body. "*Goro goro suru*" means to pass time with no particular purpose.

パタパタ [*pata pata*]：扇子であおぐ音や，紙や布などの軽い物が風にはためく音。
The sound when a fan is used or something light — a sheet of paper or cloth — is being flapped by the wind.

ニャー(オ) [*nyaa (o)*]：ネコの鳴き声。
The sound made by a meowing cat.

ゴロゴロ(④) [*goro goro*]：ネコがのどを鳴らす音。
The sound made by a purring cat.

お布団

① *poka poka* / *dosa* / *beron*
② ― Ofuton o hoshita kara attakai desho. (I've aired the bedding. Isn't it warm?)
　― **Fuka fuka no hoka hoka** da. (It's soft and warm.)
③ Hi no nioitte **honwaka** shite kimochi ga ii ne. (The "smell" of the sunshine is so warm and comforting.)
④ **suya suya**

ポカポカ [*poka poka*]：心地よい暖かさ(類：ホカホカ)。
　Feeling comfortably warm.
ドサ(ッ) [*dosa (t)*]：大きくてかさばるものが投げられたり，置かれたりした時の音。
　A thud used to express a sound produced when a big or bulky object is thrown or put into place.
ベロン [*beron*]：平たくて柔らかい物を掛ける時の音。
　When something flat or soft is hanging.
フカフカ [*fuka fuka*]：柔らかく軽い様子を表す。柔らかさ，軽さを表す「フワフワ」と比べると，「フカフカ」の方がかさがあり，弾力性も示唆している。
　Being soft and fluffy. When compared to *fuwa fuwa*, meaning soft and light, something described as *fuka fuka* has more volume and is elastic.
ホカホカ [*hoka hoka*]：暖かくて，肌に心地よい様子。
　Being warm and comfortable to the skin.
ホンワカ [*honwaka*]：心地よい温かさを表す。
　When a person feels comfortably warm.
スヤスヤ [*suya suya*]：穏やかに，心地よさげに眠る様子。同様の表現に「グッスリ」があり，こちらは深く眠る様子を表す。
　Sleeping quietly and comfortably. A similar term, *gussuri*, is used when sleeping soundly.

Various Situations

食べすぎに注意

① — **Gatsu gatsu** tabeteru! Yohodo onaka ga suiteita no ne.（She's eating like a pig! She must have been really hungry.）

② — **Maru maru** futotte **koro koro** shite kawaii desho.（She's so round and plump. Isn't she cute?）

③ — Demo, anata wa **buku buku** futorisugi! Daietto shinakya **buyo buyo** no **yore yore** ni naru wa.（But you are too fat! If you don't go on a diet, you'll get flabby and shabby.）

> **ガツガツ** [*gatsu gatsu*]：貪欲を表す。「ガツガツする」は空腹で物を食べあさる様子や貪欲に何かを求める様子。
> Greedily. *"Gatsu gatsu suru"* means that you eat like a pig or simply that you are greedy.
>
> **マルマル** [*maru maru*]：良い意味で、よく太っていることを表す。通常、犬、ネコ、赤ん坊などに使われる。
> Used in a favorable sense to describe something or someone plump. It is generally used to describe cats, puppies and babies.
>
> **コロコロ** [*koro koro*]：転がる様子。また、丸くて転がっていきそうな様子。
> Rolling. It is also used when something is so round that it looks as though it may start to roll.
>
> **ブクブク** [*buku buku*]：太っている様子。「マルマル」に比べて、軽蔑のニュアンスがある。
> Fat. Compared to *maru maru*, this word has a tone of contempt.
>
> **ブヨブヨ** [*buyo buyo*]：締まりの無い様子。
> Flabby.
>
> **ヨレヨレ** [*yore yore*]：疲れ果てた、むさ苦しい様子。元は、汚れた古着を形容する言葉だが、ひどく疲れた人の様子を表すのにも使われる。
> Worn out; shabby. Originally, this adjective was used to describe dirty old clothes, but it is also used to describe a person who is extremely tired.

安全運転

① — Mae no kuruma, sakkikara **mota mota** hashitteru …!（The car ahead of us has been dawdling for a while.）
　— Michi ni mayotteru no kana …（I wonder if the driver is lost …）
② **kurut**
　— Usetsushite chikamichi shiyo …!（Let's turn right and take a short cut.）
③ — Demo, kono roji wa kodomo ga **hyoi** to tobiderukara …（But children suddenly jump out on this road …）
　— **Noro noro** soko wa **ira ira** surukedo anzen kana?（Driving slowly irritates me but it may be safer.）

モタモタ ［*mota mota*］：遅い状態・行為に対していう表現(類: グズグズ, ノソノソ)。
Describes a condition or an action that is not swift. Synonymous with *guzu guzu* and *noso noso*.

クルッ ［*kurut*］：急な回転を表す。
Describes an abrupt turn.

ヒョイ ［*hyoi*］：予期せぬ出来事を表す。
Describes an unexpected event.

ノロノロ ［*noro noro*］：非常に遅い動きを表す。
Describes very slow movement.

イライラ ［*ira ira*］：いらだちを表す。
Describes feeling irritated.

Various Situations

軽快に

① *sui sui* / *chon chon*
② *tsuu*

スイスイ [*sui sui*]：軽快に進む様子。
An expression used to describe something nimble.

チョンチョン [*chon chon*]：小さく軽快な動きをくり返す様子。ここでは，やさしく蹴る様子。
Describes the sound of something striking repeatedly. Here the term is used to describe gentle kicking.

ツー（ッ） [*tsuu (t)*]：水滴がすべり落ちる様子など，まっすぐで滑らかな動きを表す。
This expression is used to describe smooth straight movement, like gliding drops of water.

年末は大忙し

① ― *Mada kurisumasu kado o dashite inai wa ...*（I haven't mailed any Christmas cards yet.）
　― *Watashi mo nengajo o kakanakya ...*（I have to write my New Year's cards, too.）
② ― *Kotoshi mo **atafuta** to owariso ne ...*（This year will be ending in a hurry as well, I suppose.）
③ ***gaya gaya／wai wai***
　― *Oshogatsu wa miuchi ga atsumaru kara yappari isogashi desho ...*（After all, we are busy during New Year because so many relatives get together.）
④ ― ***Hot** to suru no wa neru toki dake ...!*（The only time we can relax is when we sleep.）
　shiin

 解説

アタフタ ［*atafuta*］：忙しく，急いでいる様子。
　Busy and in a hurry.
ガヤガヤ ［*gaya gaya*］：大勢の人の声が混じり合って意味をなさない騒音となっている状態を表す。
　A situation in which the voices of many people merge into a meaningless din.
ワイワイ ［*wai wai*］：「ガヤガヤ」と同様。大勢の人の声でにぎやかな様子。
　A synonym for *gaya gaya*.
ホッ ［*hot*］：安堵のため息をつく様子。
　A sigh of relief.
シイイイン（シーン） ［*shiin*］：非常に静かな様子。
　Dead calm.

Various Situations

風をきって

解説

サアーッ（サーッ） [*saat*]：素早い動きを表す。
Describes quick movement.
ドバアアーッ（ドバーッ） [*dobaat*]：液状の物が一気に噴き出し，拡がる様子。
Describes the sudden appearance and spread of something liquid.
ピタ（ッ） [*pita (t)*]：突然の停止を表す。類義語は「ピタリ」「ピッタリ」。
Describes a sudden stop. Its synonyms are *pitari* and *pittari*.

①***saat***
— *Kaze o kitte hashiru no wa kimochi ga ii ...!* (What a pleasant feeling it is to ride fast with the breeze against me !)

②***dobaat／pita***
— *Demo teishi suru to ase ga taki no yoni ...!* (But when I stop, sweat pours off me like a waterfall.)

危険な道

 解説

スレスレ [*sure sure*]：非常に近接している様子。
Describes a situation in which something is very close to something else.

ギリギリ [*giri giri*]：何かの端や極限に近い状態を表す。
Describes something at the limit or edge.

ハラハラ [*hara hara*]：誰か，または何かの状況についての心配を表す。類義語の「ドキドキ」は，緊張，不安，期待などで心臓が激しく鼓動している様子。
Describes a feeling of apprehension over the condition of someone or something else. Its synonym, ***doki doki***, indicates one's heart is pounding due to tension, anxiety or expectation.

ヒヤヒヤ [*hiya hiya*]：危険を感じ，恐れや不安を抱いている状態を表す。
Expresses fear or anxiety, because of a sense of danger.

① — *Gake ni **sure sure** da ...!* (We're driving so close to the cliff.)
② — *Michihaba mo **giri giri** da yo!!! **Hara hara** suru ne ...* (The width of the road is almost the same as the car's. It gives me the shivers...)
③ — ***Hiya hiya** shite kimo o tsubushi so da. Kaeri wa betsu no ruto ni shiyo yo ...* (This is terrifying. Let's take a different route going home...)

中身が重要

 解説

ズッシリ [*zusshiri*]：重さのある様子。「ズシリ」の強調形。
The exaggerated form of *zushiri*, which expresses heaviness.

パラパラ [*para para*]：ページをめくったり、小石や小雨が落ちる時の音を表す。
Describes the sounds produced when someone flips pages or by falling pebbles or light rain.

ペラペラ [*pera pera*]：板切れや紙、布などが薄い様子。
Describes thin boards, paper or clothes.

① *para para*
— **Zusshiri** shita hon nano ni johoryo ga sukunai... (Although it's heavy, this book contains little information.)
② — Kore wa do daro? (How about this book?)
③ — **Pera pera** nano ni nakami ga koi! (Although it's thin, the book is informative.)

ピカピカ

ピカピカ [*pika pika*]：人や物が新しく，輝くようで，しばしば希望に満ちた様子。物を磨いた後に光る様子も表す（例：靴をピカピカに磨く，ピカピカのステンレス）。

Describes a situation or an object that is new, bright and full of hope. It also refers to something that gleams after being polished. Examples: *Kutsu o pika pika ni migaku* (I polished my shoes until they were really shiny) and *pika pika no sutenresu* (stainless steel).

① ― **Pika pika** *no ichinensei da ne …* (What a smart-looking first-year primary school student.)
② ― **Pika pika** *no shinnyu shain desu.* (We're freshmen employees.)
③ ― **Pika pika** *no shacho da.* (The president has a shiny bald head.)

Various Situations

おしゃべり

① *pecha kucha*
② *butsu butsu*
③ *hiso hiso*

解説

ペチャクチャ [*pecha kucha*]：おしゃべりが続く様子。
Describes continuous chatter.

ブツブツ [*butsu butsu*]：つぶやきを表し，しばしば否定的な含意がある(例：ブツブツ小言を言う)。
Indicates the sound of mumbling, which has a negative connotation. For example, *butsu butsu kogoto o iu* (mumbling about someone's faults).

ヒソヒソ [*hiso hiso*]：内緒話など，小声で話す様子。否定的な含意がある。
Refers to speaking in a low or hushed tone and can be used to describe the act of talking behind someone's back. The term also has a negative connotation.

汗をかいたら

ベタベタ [*beta beta*]：液体状の物で表面が粘りつく様子。
Describes a condition in which a surface is sticky with a liquidlike substance.

ジトジト [*jito jito*]：(空気中の) 湿気が多い状態を表す。
Describes a humid condition.

サッ [*sat*]：急な動き，または何かの動作を素早く終える様子。ここでは，シャワーを浴びるのにかかる時間が短い，ということを強調している。
Describes a sudden movement or the way in which someone finishes doing something abruptly. Here the term is used to emphasize that she will not take long to have a shower.

サッパリ [*sappari*]：気分が改まるようなさわやかな様子または感覚。
Refers to a fresh feeling or impression.

①— Ase de **beta beta** suru ...! (I'm dripping with sweat.)
jito jito
②— **Sat** to shawa o abiyo ... (I'll take a quick shower.)
③— Aa, **sappari** shita! (Ah! I feel so refreshed!)

Various Situations

会話はバッチリ

ペラペラ [*pera pera*]：冗舌な様子や、外国語が堪能な様子。
Describes being talkative as well as fluency in a foreign language.

スラスラ [*sura sura*]：動作などが滑らかな様子。ここでは流ちょうに読むことを指す。
Describes movements or actions that proceed smoothly. Here, it describes fluency in reading.

① — *Nihongo no kaiwa wa **pera pera** da ne …* (You can speak Japanese fluently, can't you?)
② — *Kono hon o koe o dashi te yonde goran …* (Try to read this book aloud.)
③ — ***Sura sura** yomu no wa muzukashii ne …* (It's difficult to read it out just like that.)

年賀状

シッカリ [*shikkari*]：物の形などが堅固で安定している様子。感情や性格，態度を表すことも。
Describes the condition of a firm and steadfast formation or connection. The term can also be used for feelings, personalities and behavior.

サラサラ [*sara sara*]：ここでは，手慣れた筆跡を意味している。何かをやすやすと行う様子(類: スラスラ)。
Here the term refers to skillful handwriting. It can also describe an action that proceeds without difficulty, a meaning synonymous with *sura sura*.

ヒョロヒョロ [*hyoro hyoro*]：痩せて弱々しい様子。類義語の「ヨロヨロ」はふらついている様子。
Describes something slender that looks fragile. A synonym, *yoro yoro*, describes a wobbly or loose state.

① (A couple are looking through New Year's greeting cards they have received.)
— *Kare wa itsumo* **shikkari** *shita ji o kaku ne.* (His handwriting always seems so bold and confident.)
— *Tappitsu ne.* (He's real calligrapher, isn't he?)

②— *Kono hito wa* **sara sara** *tto kaite atte moji ni aji ga aru wa …* (This person's handwriting is so smooth and fluid. It has a unique touch.)

③— *Boku no ji wa* **hyoro hyoro** *de hazukashii kara pasokon wa choho da.* (As I feel ashamed of my poor handwriting, I really appreciate my computer.)

マイホーム

ギコギコ [*giko giko*]：強い抵抗を受けながら摩擦が起きている様子。ここでは、のこぎりを引く音を表す。
Usually refers to the sound of friction with a lot of resistance. In this case, the term represents the sound of sawing.

トントン [*ton ton*]：固い物を軽く、繰り返したたく様子。
The sound of hitting something lightly over and over.

カンカン [*kan kan*]：固くて、比較的軽い金属質のものを繰り返したたく様子。
The sound of repeatedly hitting a relatively light metallic object.

コツコツ [*kotsu kotsu*]：継続的に努力するさまを表す。
Suggests one's constant efforts.

ペタペタ [*peta peta*]：平らな部分に何かをくり返し塗ったり、貼ったりする様子。ここではペンキを塗る様子。
Describes a substance being repeatedly applied to something flat. In this case, the term describes the act of spreading paint with a brush.

① ***giko giko***
② ***ton ton*／*kan kan***
③ ― Hitori de ***kotsu kotsu*** tateta maihomu da ...(This is my home that I've built by myself, little by little ....)
peta peta

さまざまな様子

リフォームどき

解説

ガタ [gata]：比較的重い物同士がぶつかり合う様子，またはその音。「ガタがくる」で接合部分などが劣化して，ドアなどが滑らかに開閉できない様子。
Describes two relatively heavy objects hitting each other or the sound made in such an event. *"Gata ga kuru"* idiomatically describes a situation in which fixtures and fittings have deteriorated and doors, for example, no longer open and close smoothly.

ギシギシ [gishi gishi]：比較的重い物がきしむ音。
A creaking or grating sound of a relatively heavy object.

パキッ [pakit]：薄くて固い物が割れたり，ひびが入る時の音。
The sound caused when a thin and hard object is broken or cracks.

メリッ [merit]：頑丈で硬い物に亀裂が入る時の音。
The sound made when solid and hard objects crack.

ミシッ [mishit]：大木や木造の家などが何らかの力を受けて，きしんだり，たわんだりする時の音。
The sound made when large trees, wooden houses or wooden objects creak or lean under pressure.

トホホ [tohoho]：落ち込んだとき，悲惨な状況に置かれた時の心理的状態。
Indicates a depressed or pitiful feeling or situation.

① — *Wagaya wa kanari **gata** ga kiteru ne ...* (My house has become quite old and rickety.)
  gishi gishi
② — *Mainichi dokoka de oto ga suru ...!* (Every day I hear noises from somewhere or other.)
  merit / pakit / mishit
③ — *Tatenaoshi no shikin wa takarakuji no tokusho o ateru shika nai ...* (To finance the rebuilding of my house, my only hope is to win the lottery's grand prize.)
  tohoho

Various Situations

子育て

キリリ [*kiriri*]：引き締まっていて，品のある様子。人間に使われる時は，賢く，生き生きとして，勇敢だ，という含意がある。
Describes something tight and dignified without looseness. When used for a person, the term suggests that they are wise, lively or brave.

メロメロ [*mero mero*]：愛情のため正常な判断能力を失っている様子。ただし，この例が示すように，好ましい様子として使われることがある。
Describes a mental condition under which one cannot function normally because of being utterly infatuated by someone or something. However, as in this case, the term may be used in a favorable context.

ズッシリ [*zusshiri*]：重さを表す。
Describes something heavy.

①― ***Kiriri*** *to shita kaodachi ne ...*（Your baby has a distinguished face.）
②― *Goshujin mo **mero mero** desho ...*（Your husband is gaga over him, isn't he?）
③― *Kono kuni no shorai ga kodomo ya oya no ryokata ni **zusshiri** noshikakatte iru wa ...*（The future of the nation rests on the shoulders of children like him, and their parents, too.）
―*Minna de sapoto shinakya ...*（Everybody has to help them [with child care].）

お届け物

ピンポーン（ピンポン）[*pin pon*]：玄関などの呼び鈴が鳴る音。
The sound a doorbell makes.

ドカッ[*dokat*]：大きくて重い物が勢いよく置かれる様子，またはその音を表す。そこから派生して，お金や注文，雪など，何か大量の物が一挙にもたらされる様子を表すこともある。
Describes a large, heavy mass falling onto something, or a similar sound. By extension, the term also can suggest a large amount of something —such as money, orders or snow— gathering all at once.

ドッサリ[*dossari*]：大量，多量。
Plentiful.

① ***pin pon***
— *Haai.* (Yes.)
② — *Takuhaibin desu.* (I have a delivery for you.)
— *Gokurosama.* (Thank you.)
dokat
③ — *Obaachan kara yasai ga **dossari** todoita wa.* (Grandma has sent us a ton of vegetables.)

温泉気分

タップリ [*tappuri*]：必要以上に多い様子。
Suggests there is plenty of something.

ドップリ [*doppuri*]：何かが水などに浸かっている様子。比喩的に，何かに夢中の状態を表すこともある。
Indicates something is soaked, or, figuratively speaking, someone is hooked on something.

チョロチョロ [*choro choro*]：少量の水が蛇口から出る音。
The sound of a small amount of water coming out of a faucet.

ザザザ [*za za za*]：ここでは，大量の水が湯船からあふれ出る音を表している。「ザーザー」ならどしゃ降りの雨や早い水の流れを表す。
In this scene, it's a sound describing a relatively large amount of water overflowing from the bathtub. *Zaa zaa* is the sound of heavy rain or fast-running water.

パシャ [*pasha*]：水のはねる音。
The sound of splashing water.

①— *Onsenkibun de **tappuri** no oyu ni shiyo …* (Let's fill it up to the top for that hot-spring feeling …)
②— *Ii kibun da.* (This feels wonderful.)
　doppuri／choro choro／za za za
③— *Oyu o dashippanashi ni shinai de ne …!* (Don't leave the water running!)
　pasha

春

① — *Tsubomi ga* **fukkura** *fukuran de ... haru da ne.* (This bud is getting fat. Spring has come.)
   pachit
② — *Hora, koko ni mo* **hyokkori** *me ga deteru!* (Look, a bud is emerging here all of a sudden, too.)
   — *Kochira no wakaba wa* **muku muku** *sodatteru yo! Papa.* (These new leaves are getting big, daddy!)
③ — *Nikibi mo* **butsu butsu** *fueso da ne.* (So are your pimples.)

フックラ [*fukkura*]：やわらかく膨らんだ様子。
   Plump.
パチッ [*pachit*]：カメラのシャッターが降りる音。
   The sound of a camera's shutter.
ヒョッコリ [*hyokkori*]：偶然に思いかけず出会ったり，現れたりする様子。
   An adverb to describe an unexpected encounter with a person, or a person unexpectedly appearing.
ムクムク [*muku muku*]：柔らかなものが成長し大きくなる様子。
   Describes something soft that becomes big or fat.
ブツブツ [*butsu butsu*]：にきびなど粒状のものを表す。
   Describes something lumpy, like a skin rash or pimples.

スポーツ観戦 1

① — *Kono batta mo **chon** to aterunoga umai ... Sorede rui o umete ...*（This batter is good at hitting the ball lightly...then he fills the bases）

waat

— *Tsugi no batta ga **katsun** to taimuri hitto o utsu. Koshite **choro choro** to ten o kaseideiku.*（The next batter strikes clear clutch hits, and so he gradually piles up runs.）

— ***Dokan** to homuran de ten o torareruyorimo, shubi no ho wa shinriteki ni tsukareru de shone.*（If they score like that, the fielders will get more tired mentally than if they hit a home run.）

② **gakut**

— *Mata utareta ...! Pitcha wa kotai desu ne.*（Another hit! The pitcher should be changed.）

チョン [*chon*]：小さく軽快な動作を表す。
Describes a motion that is light.

ワーッ [*waat*]：大きな歓声を表す。
Vociferous cheers.

カツン [*katsun*]：ここでは，ボールをバットで軽く打つ音（類: コツン）。
In this situation, it describes the sound of lightly hitting a ball with a bat. Synonymous with *kotsun*.

チョロチョロ [*choro choro*]：水が少しずつ流れる様子，またはその音。ここでは少しずつ点をかせぐこと
The sound or state of a little water flowing. In this situation, it means runs come gradually, like a continuous trickle of water.

ドカン [*dokan*]：爆発音。ここではホームランを表す。「ドカンと一発」はよく使われる表現。
The sound of an explosion. In this situation, it is used to describe hitting a home run. The expression "*dokan to ippatsu*" is commonly used in baseball.

ガクッ [*gakut*]：落胆を表す。「ガックリ」も同義。
Describes disappointment. Synonymous with *gakkuri*.

スポーツ観戦２

① ― **Bun bun** furimawasu dake nara kodomo ni datte dekiru ...!（Even a young child can swing a bat around!）
　byun／spot
②**ira ira**
　― Ano kamaekata ga yokunai ...（His batting stance is no good.）
③**sukaan**
　― Utta ...! Homuran da ...! Kore de **sukat** to shita ...!（He did it! It's a home run! That's a relief!）

ブンブン［*bun bun*］：棒状のものを振り回す様子，またはその音（類：ビュンビュン）。ここでは，バットをやみくもに振る様子を表す。
The term describes a situation in which a person is swinging around a sticklike object and the sound heard in such a situation. In this case, it refers to the pointless swinging of the bat, ***byun byun*** is its synonym.

ビュン［*byun*］：空気を切り裂くように進む音。
The sound of something speedily zipping through the air.

スポッ［*spot*］：早く動く物があるものにはまる様子。あるいは，逆にそのような物が瞬間的に解放される様子。あるいはその音。
Describes a situation in which a fast-moving object is trapped or when an object suddenly is released at high speed. It also describes the sound produced in such a situation.

イライラ［*ira ira*］：いら立ちを表す。
Expresses an irritated feeling.

スカーン［*sukaan*］：ここでは，バットがボールに完璧な当たりを見せる様子。
In this case, it describes the sound of the bat making perfect contact with the ball.

スカッ［*sukat*］：心が解放された様子。
Expresses a feeling of relief.

| Various Situations

スポーツ観戦 3

解説

グイグイ [*gui gui*]：何かを繰り返し力一杯押す、または引く様子。ここでは、試合で相手にプレッシャーをかけ続けることを表す。
Describes the action of repeatedly pushing or pulling something with all one's might. In this situation, it means keeping up pressure in a game.

ワ(ァ)ーワ(ァ)ー [*waa waa*]：大声を出して騒いでいる様子。ここでは観衆の応援の声。
Describes a loud noise made by a crowd. Here, it describes the noise made by the cheering crowd at a soccer game.

ウワァッ（ウワーッ） [*uwaat*]：大きな驚き、またはそれを表す声。
Expressing great surprise or the sound of expressing it.

ガクッ [*gakut*]：失望で力を失う様子。
In this case, the term refers to losing one's energy due to disappointment. *Gakkuri* is a synonym.

プチッ [*puchit*]：リモコンを使ってテレビを消す音。
The sound of turning off a television using a remote control.

① — ... *Ike, ike!* **Gui gui** *oshite ike* ...!! (Go, go! Come on!)
waa waa

② — *Dotanba made oitsumeta noni gyakutenmake da!* (We had them beaten, but they came back and scored a last-minute victory!)
uwaat

③ **gakut** / **puchit**

Chapter 2

Various Movements

いろいろな動き

Various Movements

動かないで

① *jii*
② —*Motto raku ni shite.* (Relax a little more.)
　jii
③ —*Sugu owaru kara jit to shite ne.* (This won't take long, so please sit still.)
④ *jirot*
　—*Jit to shite!!!* (Stand still!)

ジィ（ジッ）[*jii(jit)*]：動かず静かにしている様子や，立ちつくす様子。不安や興奮，期待などから息を凝らす状態を表すことも。「ジーッ」なら長い間動きを止めていることを表す。「ジッと」であれば，短い間の，または強度の不安，期待，関心などを表す。
Being motionless or quiet, or standing still. It is also used to convey the idea of holding one's breath in suspense, excitement or expectation. *Jiit* expresses the idea of being motionless for a long time. If ji is pronounced *jit to*, it shows a brief period or strong level of suspense, excitement or interest.

ジロッ[*jirot*]：悪意ある目つきを表す。「ジロジロ」なら人を好奇心などから見回す様子。いずれも肯定的なニュアンスはない。
Giving a baleful look at something or someone. *jiro jiro* means looking someone up and down with curiosity. None of these words have a favorable connotation.

あやしい人物

① *kyoro kyoro*
② *uro uro*
③ *biku biku* ／ *oro oro*

解説

キョロキョロ [*kyoro kyoro*]：四方を見回す様子。
　Looking every which way.
ウロウロ [*uro uro*]：落ち着き無くうろつく様子。「うろたえる」から派生した語。
　Loitering in a restless manner; a derivative of *"urotaeru"* (becoming confused).
ビクビク [*biku biku*]：神経質に何かを恐れている様子。
　Nervous; fearful.
オロオロ [*oro oro*]：慌て，混乱し，どうしていいかわからない様子。
　Flustered; not knowing what to do.

Various Movements

どちらの方が

① **kiko kiko / sui sui**
— Maika yori jitensha de dekakeru ho ga undo busoku ni naranai. (It's better to use my bike rather than take the car — that way I get sufficient exercise.)

② **suta suta**
— Jitensha yori toho ga muri naku ase o nagasete kenko ni ii. (Walking is better than riding a bike. I work up a sweat much easier that way.)

③ **shito shito**
— Ame no hi wa... (And on rainy days...)

④ **jit**
— Ie ni ita ho ga okane o tsukawazu ni sumu. (...it's better to stay at home — that way I won't have to spend any money.)

解説

キコキコ [*kiko kiko*]：金属がきしむ音。自転車のペダルがきしんで，油を差す必要がある様子を表す。

The sound of metallic objects creaking. The expression is used to refer to the sound of a bicycle's pedals that need to be oiled.

スイスイ [*sui sui*]：軽やかに進む様子。

This term is used to refer to something moving lightly.

スタスタ [*suta suta*]：きびきびと歩く様子。リズム感のある足音を表している。

This term is used to refer to someone walking at a brisk pace. It describes the sound of rhythmic footsteps.

シトシト [*shito shito*]：弱い雨が降る音。

This term describes light rainfall.

ジッ [*jit*]：動かない様子。

This term is used to refer to a situation in which people or animals are motionless.

力持ち

① — Kore, mochiagerareru?（Can you lift this?）
② **hyoi**
　— Karui mon sa...!（No problem.）
③ **dosun**
　— Orosu no wa ranbo da ne...（Came down roughly, didn't it?）

解説

ヒョイ [*hyoi*]：軽々と持ち上げる様子。
Expresses an act of lifting something easily.
ドスン [*dosun*]：重い物が落ちた音。
The sound of something heavy falling.

Various Movements

歩き方

① *yochi yochi* / *chima chima*

② ― Ano **fura fura** no yopparai, uchi no oyaji ja nai koto o negau yo... （I hope that reeling drunk isn't my father.）
yoro yoro / **yota yota**

解説

ヨチヨチ [*yochi yochi*]：しっかり歩くことができない様子。小さい歩幅で歩く様子。幼児が歩く様子を表す典型的な表現。

Describes being unable to walk steadily, or taking small steps. A typical expression used to describe the way toddlers walk.

チマチマ [*chima chima*]：小さな動き。この場合は小さな歩幅で歩く様子。

Refers to small-scale activity ― in this case, taking short steps.

フラフラ [*fura fura*]：おぼつかない動き，または状態（例：フラフラした生き方）。

Describes a flailing motion. The term also can be used to refer to a state or condition ― for example, *fura fura shita ikikata* (an unstable lifestyle).

ヨロヨロ [*yoro yoro*]：疲労やショック，酒酔い，体力の喪失などでぐったりした様子を表す。足元がおぼつかない様子を特徴とする状態。

Describes someone who looks worn out due to exhaustion, shock, intoxication or loss of physical strength. Often characterized by stumbling.

ヨタヨタ [*yota yota*]：不安定に揺れながら進む様子。「ヨチヨチ」も「ヨタヨタ」と同様の動きを表すが，前者は主に幼い子ども，後者は本来しっかり歩ける人（がそうできない時）に使う。

Refers to walking unsteadily. Although both *yochi yochi* and *yota yota* indicate a similar walking action, the former is used mainly for young children, while the latter is used for people who should be able to walk properly.

並ぶより…

① **zoro zoro**
② **suut**
③ **hyoi hyoi**
― Kaidan ga hirokute hayai...! (The stairs are wider and faster!)

ゾロゾロ [*zoro zoro*]：群衆が立てる音，または大勢の人間がゆっくり動く時に立てる音。
Refers to the sound of a crowd or the slow movement made by a lot of people.

スーッ [*suut*]：人や物が静かに動く音。
Expresses the silent movement of a person or an object.

ヒョイヒョイ [*hyoi hyoi*]：「ヒョイ」は勢いのある身軽な動き。ここでは連続して跳ねる様子(顣: ピョンピョン)。「ヒョイヒョイ」は次のような場合にも使う(例: どこへでも気軽にヒョイヒョイ出かける)。
Hyoi describes swift movement. Here, ***hyoi hyoi*** indicates an act of several jumps in succession, with its synonym **pyon pyon**. ***Hyoi hyoi*** can also be used as in the following example. *Doko e demo kigaruni* ***hyoi hyoi*** *dekakeru*. This emphasizes that the person does not hesitate at all about going out anywhere or anytime.

Various Movements

休日

ゴロゴロ [*goro goro*]：大きな物が転がる様子。ここでは，人が寝転がって何もしない状態を表している。

Indicates a large object rolling around. Here it describes the man sitting around the house.

ムックリ [*mukkuri*]：突然起き上がる様子。

Describes the act of sitting upright suddenly.

ブラブラ [*bura bura*]：この場合は，目的もなく歩き回る様子。時間を無為に過ごす状態を表すこともも(例：失業中で毎日ブラブラしている)。

In this situation, the term refers to walking around aimlessly. Bura bura can also be used as a nuance for passing the day idly. For example, *Shitsugyo chu de mainichi **bura bura** shite iru* (I'm between jobs, so I just do nothing every day).

① — ***Goro goro** shite inai de sanpo shite kitara?* (Why don't you stop lounging about and go for a walk?)

② ***mukkuri***
— *Mokuteki mo naku aruku no wa nigate nan dakedo...* (I don't like walking around aimlessly.)

③ ***bura bura***
— *Ie ni iru to gomi atsukai da na...* (I'm treated like dirt when I'm at home.)

いろいろな動き

うたたね

① *uto uto*
② *kokkuri kokkuri*
③ *hat ／ kyoton ／ bikut*

解説

ウトウト [*uto uto*]：居眠りしている状態を表す。
Describes a situation in which one is slumbering.

コックリコックリ [*kokkuri kokkuri*]：眠りながら首を縦に振る状態。
Means nodding off to sleep.

ハッ [*hat*]：ここでは，赤ちゃんが突然目を覚ます様子。驚きや突然のショックで人が緊張し，一瞬息を止める様子を表すことも。
In this situation, the term describes a baby who is startled awake. The term also refers to a situation in which a surprise or sudden shock causes a person to tense up and momentarily stop breathing.

キョトン [*kyoton*]：突然起こされたり，驚かされたりした後，放心している様子。短時間虚をつかれている様子を表す。「ポカン」も同義。
Describes a state of disorientation after being suddenly awoken or startled. The term suggests a short-lived blank state of mind. Its synonyms is *pokan*.

ビクッ [*bikut*]：驚きで一瞬体をこわばらせる様子。
The term describes one becoming astonished and stiffening.

Various Movements

冷たい雨

① *shobo shobo* / *gata gata*
— *Samui!* (It's cold!)
② *wana wana*
③ *burut*

解説

ショボショボ [*shobo shobo*]：弱い雨が絶え間なく降る様子。
Describes a situation in which a small amount of rain is falling continuously.

ガタガタ [*gata gata*]：弱い揺れや震えが続く様子。または、その音。
Describes continuous small shakes or quivers. Also indicates the associated sounds.

ワナワナ [*wana wana*]：「ガタガタ」の類義語で、怒りや寒さ、病気、恐怖などで震えが抑えられない様子。
A synonym of *gata gata*, the term suggests shaking in a more uncontrollable way for such reasons as anger, coldness, sickness or fear.

ブルッ [*burut*]：強い震えを表す。
Describes a much stronger shaking motion, or being all aquiver.

動きいろいろ

(panel 1) 蝶は舞い…　ひら　ひら
(panel 2) トンボは飛び…　スイ　スイ
(panel 3) 蛙は跳ね…　ピョン　ピョン
(panel 4) 人は水溜りを避けて…　ヒョイ　ヒョイ

① **hira hira**
— Cho wa mai... (The butterfly is fluttering about.)
② **sui sui**
— Tonbo wa tobi... (The dragonfly is flitting.)
③ **pyon pyon**
— Kaeru wa hane... (The frog is hopping.)
④ **hyoi hyoi**
— Hito wa mizutamari o sakete... (The man is jumping to avoid puddles.)

解説

ヒラヒラ [*hira hira*]：軽く薄い物が風に吹かれている，または，はためいている様子。葉や花びらが地面に落ちる様子も表す。

Describes a situation in which a light, thin object is blown in the wind or such an object is fluttering. *Hira hira* is typically used to describe falling leaves or flower petals.

スイスイ [*sui sui*]：滑らかな動きや，物事が何の抵抗もなく進行している状態。「仕事がスイスイはかどる」のような例で使う。

Describes a smooth movement and progress without resistance. The term can be used in a situation like "*shigoto ga sui sui hakadoru*" (doing pretty well in one's work).

ピョンピョン [*pyon pyon*]：動物や昆虫などが跳びはねる様子。

Refers to animals and insects jumping around.

ヒョイヒョイ [*hyoi hyoi*]：身軽で素早い動きを表す。

Suggests nimble movements.

気分転換

解説

ダラーン [*daraan*]：物が寄りかかったり，垂れ下がったりしている様子。ここでは無気力な様子。
Describes a situation in which something is slumped or dangling. Here it describes a feeling of not wanting to do anything at all.

シャキッ [*shakkit*]：緊張し，引き締まった感じを表す。
Describes a tense, uptight feeling.

ブラッ [*burat*]：目的無く歩く様子。「ブラブラ」と類義。
Describes the act of walking aimlessly. Its synonym is *bura bura*.

ノコノコ [*noko noko*]：不適切なタイミングで出かけること。または，他人の当惑をよそに不適当な時に姿を現すこと。この例の場合は，大事な仕事を残して出かけてしまう様子を表している。
Describes a situation in which someone goes out at an inappropriate moment, or shows up at an inopportune moment much to the irritation of others. In this case, it describes the man's act of leaving his work although it is important.

① *daraan*
② — Kibun ga **shakit** to shinai... (I can't get into this...)
③ — **Burat** to sanpo demo shite koyo... (I think I'll go for a walk.)
  noko noko

あきらめない

何度もつまずき、何度こけても…

しっかりしろ!

めげずに起きあがり助けあって…

見えないゴールを目指すのが人生…!?

解説

ドテッ [*dotet*]：比較的重い人や動物が倒れる音。
Describes the sound of a relatively heavy person or animal falling over.

シッカリ [*shikkari*]：堅固で安定している状態を表す。
Describes something solid and stable.

グイッ [*guit*]：力のこもった素早い動きを表す。この場合は，男性がもう一人の男性を引っ張る様子を表している。
Describes a powerful action or movement done quickly. In this case, the term describes the man pulling the other man up.

ムックリ [*mukkuri*]：大きくて重い物が，横になった状態から起き上がる様子を表す。
Deseribes a large, heavy object that had been lying flat being raised.

ハアハア [*haa haa*]：息切れしている様子。
Describes breathing in short gasps.

ヨタヨタ [*yota yota*]：よろめいたり，つまずきながら歩く様子(類：ヨロヨロ，フラフラ)。
Describes a waddling or stumbling gait. ***Yoro yoro*** and ***fura fura*** are synonyms.

① ***dotet***
— *Nando mo tsumazuki, nando kokete mo...* (No matter how often I stumble and fall...)

② — ***Shikkari** shiro!* (Come on!)
guit／mukkuri
— *Megezu ni okiagari, tasuke atte...* (I mustn't feel defeated, but should pick myself up again, if necessary with help from others...)

③ ***haa haa／yota yota***
— *Mienai goru o mezasu no ga jinsei...!?* (... and keep running toward a goal I cannot see. Is this what life is about?)

Various Movements

気になる

①「…危機が**ひたひた**と迫ってくるところでCMか…!」
ドキドキ

②「トイレに行くのは今のうちだ"!」
サッ

③「…まだCMをやってる***!!!***」
タタタッ

解説

ヒタヒタ [*hita hita*]：波が打ち寄せるように，少しずつ静かに近づく様子。
Suggests something approaching little by little and quietly, like water lapping against something.

ドキドキ [*doki doki*]：興奮で心臓が鼓動する様子。
Describes a heart beating with excitement.

サッ [*sat*]：素早く，勢いのある動き。
Indicates a quick dashing movement.

タタタッ [*tatatat*]：軽い足取りで走る様子，またはその音。
Describes running with light steps or the sound of such footsteps.

① — *… Kiki ga **hita hita** to semattekuru tokoro de shiemu ka…!* (Just as we reach the critical point we have a commercial break…)
   doki doki
② ***sat***
   — *Toire ni iku no wa ima no uchi da!* (Now's the time to go to the bathroom!)
③ ***tatatat***
   — *… Mada shiemu o yatteru!!!* (The ads still on?!)

いろいろな動き

人ごみ

解説

ザワザワ [*zawa zawa*]：大勢の人が話したり動いたりする様子や音。
Describes sounds of a mixture of people talking and moving.

ゾロゾロ [*zoro zoro*]：大勢の人（この場合は歩行者）が連れだって動く様子。
Describes a large group—in this case, pedestrians—moving.

セカセカ [*seka seka*]：せわしく落ち着きのない様子。
Indicates bustling and unsettled behavior.

クタクタ [*kuta kuta*]：疲れ，弱った様子。
Describes a tired and weak, worn-out feeling.

① *zawa zawa / zoro zoro*
— Kono ekimae wa itsumo konzatsu shiteru... (The streets in front of this station are always crowded.)

② — ***Seka seka*** *aruku hito mo oi...* (Many people are walking in a hurry...)

③ *kuta kuta*
— Kono nagare ni awasete aruku no wa tsukareru yo... (It's tiring to walk at the same pace as everyone else.)

Various Movements

お互いに

ゴロゴロしてないでウォーキングでもすれば？

セカセカ

ズズズ

ぼくに内緒で何か食べてるな！

パクパク

ヌッ

体脂肪と血圧に **ビクビク** だね…

グラグラ

① — **Goro goro** shite nai de wokingu demo sureba? (How about going for a walk instead of just loafing around?)
　seka seka／zu zu zu
② **paku paku／nut**
　— Boku ni naisho de nanika tabeteru na! (I see you're eating something in secret!)
③ — Taishibo to ketsuatsu ni **biku biku** da ne… (It's frightening to find out about your body fat and blood pressure.)
　gura gura

解説

ゴロゴロ [*goro goro*]：大きなものが転がっている様子。ここでは，人が寝転がって何もしない状態を表している。
Usually refers to the sound made when a large object is rolling over. The term also can describe someone just lying down and doing nothing. as.

セカセカ [*seka seka*]：落ち着きなく動き回る様子。
Describes the act of moving around in a restless manner.

ズズズ [*zu zu zu*]：掃除機で吸いこむ音。
The sound of vacuuming a room.

パクパク [*paku paku*]：金魚のように口を開け閉めしながら食べ物を詰め込み，食べる様子。
Describes gobbling or munching, opening and closing one's mouth like a goldfish.

ヌッ [*nut*]：突然何かが姿を表す様子。
Describes a situation in which something is suddenly noticed.

ビクビク [*biku biku*]：恐れの感情を表す。
Refers to a feeling of alarm.

グラグラ [*gura gura*]：揺れている様子を表す。
Describes something reeling or shaking.

写真撮影

チョコン [*chokon*]：小さな生き物が一人で座っている様子。物にも使える。
Describes a small animate object sitting still all by itself. It also can be used for an inanimate object.

ジッ [*jit*]：動かない様子。
Refers to motionlessness.

カシャ [*kasha*]：シャッターを押す音を表現するのによく使われる。
A typical sound for releasing the shutter.

チャン [*chan*]：理想的な状態を表す。
Suggests an ideal situation or condition.

① — **Chokon** to suwatte iru tokoro o toru yo.（I'm taking a photo of you sitting in a lovely way.）
② — **Jit** to shitete ne...（Please be still.）
   kashat
③ — Hora, **chan** to toreteru. Dejitaru kamera wa sugu kakunin dekiru ne...（See? I took it right. With a digital camera, we can check how it came out right away.）

Various Movements

地震

① **gura gura / yusa yusa**
— ... *Jishin da!* (It's an earthquake!)
② **yura yura**
— ... *Osamatta na... Terebi o tsuke yo...!* (It's subsiding. Let's turn on the TV.)
③ — *Chiisakute **hot** to shita! Jishin to taifu no nai tokoro e hikkoshitai mono da...* (What a relief that the quake was a small one. I want to move to a place that won't get hit by earthquakes or typhoons.)
yare yare

解説

グラグラ [*gura gura*]：物や心理状態など，堅固であるべきものが不安定に揺れている状態。この例では，地震で部屋の中が揺れている状態を表している。湯が沸いている状態にも使うことができる。
Describes something that is supposed to be solid—physical objects or feelings—swinging unsteadily. In this case, the term describes the inside of the room shaking due to the earthquake. *Gura gura* can also be used for water that is boiling.

ユサユサ [*yusa yusa*]：大きくて，重い物がゆっくり大きく揺れている様子。
Indicates that something large and heavy is swinging slowly and widely.

ユラユラ [*yura yura*]：空気中や水中で物が揺れている様子。
Describes something waving slowly in the air or in the water.

ホッ [*hot*]：安心した様子を表す。
Expresses relief.

ヤレヤレ [*yare yare*]：安心した時，疲れた時，あるいは当惑した時の感嘆詞。
An exclamation used when someone feels relieved, tired or embarrassed.

ボール遊び

> **解説**
>
> **ポイ**［*poi*］：小さくて軽いものを放り投げる様子。「ポイ捨て」はゴミやタバコの吸い殻を放り捨てること（例：タバコのポイ捨てはやめましょう）。
>
> Describes tossing something small and light. *Poi* sute refers to throwing away trash or a cigarette butt. For example, *Tabako no poi sute wa yamemasho* means "Don't discard your cigarette butts on the road."
>
> **コロコロ**［*koro koro*］：小さくて丸い物が転がる様子。「コロ」「コロリ」「コロン」はいずれも一回の回転を表す。「コロン」はその中でも勢いが若干強い。
>
> Describes something small and round being turned over and over. *Koro*, *korori* and *koron* suggest that something is rolled only once, with *koron* indicating a roll with a slightly stronger momentum.
>
> **スイーッ**［*suiit*］：素早い動きを表す「スイ」の強調形。「スイスイ」は物事が障害や困難なく順調に進む様子。
>
> *Sui* describes a fast, quick action, with *suiit* as an exaggerated form. *Sui sui* suggests that things are going smoothly, without barriers or difficulties.

①*poi*
　— *Ei!*（Yay!）
②*koro koro*
③*suiit*
　— *A!*（Ah!）

Various Movements

ティッシュあそび

① **poi／surut**
— *Omoshiroi ne. Don don dete kuru yo...!* (This is fun. They're coming out one after another.)

② **fuwa fuwa／hira hira**
— *Mada mada...* (Still more...)

③ — *Mo nai...!?* (No more...!?)

解説

ポイ [*poi*]：小さくて軽いものを放り投げる様子。あまり深い考えもなくそうしている、という含意がある。
Describes an act of throwing something small and light, with the nuance that the person is doing so with little consideration.

スルッ [*surut*]：素早く、滞りない動きが、強い力を加えることなく起こっている様子。「スルスル」は、そのようにして物事が滑ったり、進んだりする様子。
Indicates that something moves quickly and smoothly without requiring much force. *Suru suru* describes how something slips or progresses in that way.

ドンドン [*don don*]：中断や躊躇なく物事が進む様子。
Describes the way something keeps progressing without a break or hesitation.

フワフワ [*fuwa fuwa*]：軽くて柔らかい物や、このイラストのように、そうしたものが空気中や水中で漂っている状態を表す。
Describes something very light and soft. It also is used to describe the way such objects are floating in the air or water, just like this scene.

ヒラヒラ [*hira hira*]：薄く軽いものが不規則に動く様子。ここでは、ティッシュが舞い落ちる様子。
Describes something thin and light moving randomly. In this scene, the term refers to the way tissues are fluttering down.

歯みがき粉

解説

ギューッ [*gyuut*]：何かを絞り出す音。Describes someone or something being squeezed.

ニューッ [*nyuut*]：クリームやジェルなど，柔らかくてどろどろした物がチューブなどの細い口から出てくる様子。人や幽霊，ヘビなどの長いものが隠れて居た場所から突然頭を出す様子を表すこともある。

Usually represents cream, gel or something soft and slimy coming out of a tube or a narrow gap. It also is used to depict the sudden emergence of the head of people, ghosts or long things, such as snakes, from hiding.

① — *Hamigaki, mo nai yo...*（We're out of toothpaste...）

② — *Mada nokotteru! **gyuut** to shibotte ageru.*（There's still a little left! I'll squeeze it out for you.）

③ ***nyuut***
  — *Hora, dete kita desho.*（See, it's coming out.）
  — *Minna, dete koi!*（All of it, out!）

Chapter 3

Cooking & Food
料理・食べもの

包丁

Cooking & Food

① **basat**
② — Ha o toidara **supat** to kireru yoni natta wa.（After I sharpened the kitchen knife, it cut really well.）
③ **saku saku** ／ **ton ton** ／ **gutsu gutsu**

解説

バサッ ［*basat*］：比較的大きなものを一気に切る音。
Sound of slicing something relatively large in one go.

スパッ ［*supat*］：よく切れる状態を表す。
Sound of something being cut well.

サクサク ［*saku saku*］：野菜など繊維質のものを軽快に切る時の音。
This is also a sound made when cutting something fibrous such as vegetables.

トントン ［*ton ton*］：軽くて固いものが打ちあたる音。ここではまな板の上で物を切る音。
Sound of something light and hard being hit. Here, something being chopped on a board.

グツグツ ［*gutsu gutsu*］：物が煮える音。
Used when something is at the boil or bubbling.

料理・食べもの

食べ方

① **goku goku**
② **gatsu gatsu**
— Nomimono ya tabemono no komasharu de oto o tatete nondari, taberu no ga fueta wa ne. (More and more TV food and drink commercials are showing people slurping while they eat and drink.)
③ **tsurut**
— Menrui wa susutte taberu no ga Nihonshiki daro kedo oto wa saisho ga mana da yone. (It is Japanese custom to eat noodles by slurping them, which is noisy. But it is also good to keep the noise to a minimum.)
④ **zu zu zu / mut**
— Misoshiru wa Nihon datte oto o tatecha dame! (You shouldn't make a noise while eating miso soup, though.)
Komasharu ga Nihon no mana o kaeso da! (I think commercials are changing Japanese manners.)

解説

ゴクゴク [*goku goku*]：飲み物を勢いよく飲む時にのどが立てる音。
Gulping; a gurgle in the throat.
ガツガツ [*gatsu gatsu*]：貪欲に食べる様子。
Hungrily; eating like a horse.
ツルッ [*tsurut*]：めん類などが滑らかに口の中に滑り込む時の音。
The sound made when noodles slip smoothly into the mouth.
ズズズ [*zu zu zu*]：汁をすする音。
The sound of sipping soup.
ムッ [*mut*]：不機嫌, 立腹した状態を表す。
Feeling vexed; sullen.

料理のしかた

① — **Gutsu gutsu** ninai de! Hi ga tooreba ii wa.（Don't boil that. It just needs to be heated.）
② **mogu mogu**
— Kore wa **saku saku** shita hagotae ga miryoku yo.（I like this food because of the crispy feel it has on the teeth.）
— Shita zawari mo ii ne.（It's also pleasant on the tongue.）
③ — Sore wa **chin** suru dake!（All you need to do is microwave it.）
Kore wa **sat** to yu o tooshite ne.（But for this one, it's best to run some hot water on it.）
④ — Sa, **mori mori** taberu zo!（It's time to eat!）
— Kono ato, shokki arai no yoryo mo oshienakya.（I must teach him how to do the dishes after this.）

解説

グツグツ [*gutsu gutsu*]：物が煮立つ音。
Boiling; simmering.

モグモグ [*mogu mogu*]：食べ物をかむ様子を表す。
Munching.

サクサク [*saku saku*]：砕けやすい状態を表す。クッキーの歯ごたえの例えとしてよく使われる。
A crispy feel on the teeth. It is often used when describing the texture of cookies.

チン（する） [*chin(suru)*]：電子レンジのスイッチが切れる音が語源。そこから、電子レンジで解凍、または加熱することを意味するようになった。
This word originally comes from the sound a microwave oven makes when it turns off. It now means to defrost or cook something using a microwave oven.

サッ [*sat*]：素早い動きを表す。
Quick action.

モリモリ [*mori mori*]：食欲や仕事への意欲が増大している様子。
Used to describe a person's growing appetite for food or willingness to work.

料理・食べもの

鍋の季節

① gutsu gutsu
② ― Korekara wa nabe-ryori no shizun ne.
 (This is the time of year for nabe [food cooked in one pot].)
 ― Karada ga **hoka hoka** suru. (It warms up my inside.)
③ **suya suya**
 ― Ato wa **gussuri** neru dake …!? (Afterward, I just sleep like a log.)

グツグツ [*gutsu gutsu*]：食べ物が煮える音。
　The sound of hot food being cooked.
ホカホカ [*hoka hoka*]：暖かい状態を表す。
　Condition of being warm.
グッスリ [*gussuri*]：熟睡している様子。
　State of deep sleep.
スヤスヤ [*Suya suya*]：眠っている人の静かな寝息（いびきではない）。
　Quiet breathing of a sleeper (not snoring).

Cooking & Food

食事の音

① **zu zu zu / fuu fuu**
— *Nihonjin ga oto o tatete nomu riyu no hitotsu wa ...* （One of the reasons Japanese people make a noise when they drink...）
② — *Supu-rui ga itsumo atsui kara da ...! Misoshiru mo* **atsu atsu** *ga oishi kedo ...* （is because soup is always hot ...! Hot miso soup is tasty, but ...）
③ — *Tsumetai gohan ni kakete ...* （Pour it over cold rice ...）
④ **sara sara**
— *Yappari oto wa, deru na ...* （It still makes a noise ...）

解説

ズズズ [*zu zu zu*]：汁をすする音。
The sound of sipping soup.
フーフー [*fuu fuu*]：熱い物を吹く音。
The act of blowing.
アツアツ [*atsu atsu*]：非常に熱い状態を表す（特にできたての料理）。
Describes something very hot (especially just-cooked food).
サラサラ [*sara sara*]：物が軽く流れる様子。ここでは，ご飯をみそ汁で口に流し込む音を表す。
The sound of something flowing lightly. In this situation, it describes the state and sound of washing down the rice with miso soup.

料理・食べもの

プリン

①プディングと呼ぶのが正しいけど日本語ではプリン
②プリンとしてるからね

① — *Pudingu to yobu no ga tadashikedo nihongo de wa purin.* (In English, this is called pudding, but we call it purin in Japanese.)
② — ***Purin** to shiteru kara ne.* (Because it looks "purin" [soft and wobbly].)

解説

プリン [*purin*]：やわらかく弾力性がある様子(例: 健康な赤ちゃんのお尻はプリンとしてかわいい)。類義語の「プルン」は揺れる様子を表す。

A state of being elastic. For example, *Kenko na akachan no oshiri wa **purin** to shite kawai* (The bottom of a healthy baby is wobbly and cute.) The synonymous expression ***purun*** describes a state of wobbling or trembling.

じっくり煮こんで

① いろんな具を たっぷり 入れて…
② とろ火で じっくり 煮込みましょう
③ 具が トロトロ に なったら できあがり…！
④ からだが ホカホカ あたたまるわよ / おいしそう…！

① — *Ironna gu o **tappuri** irete ...* (Let's add a lot of ingredients ...)
② — *Torobi de **jikkuri** nikomimasho.* (Simmer thoroughly over a low heat.)
   pot
③ — *Gu ga **toro toro** ni nattara dekiagari ...!* (The dish is ready when the ingredients become tender.)
④ **gokut**
   — *Karada ga **hoka hoka** atatamaru wa yo.* (The dish will warm you up.)
   — *Oishiso ...!* (It looks delicious!)

解説

タップリ [*tappuri*]：豊富にある様子。
Describes having an abundance of something.

ジックリ [*jikkuri*]：十分時間をかけて徹底的に行う様子。
Taking ample time to perform something thoroughly.

ポッ [*pot*]：小さな火や明かりをつける音。
The sound of a small flame being lit or a light being turned on.

トロトロ [*toro toro*]：滑らかで，ほとんど液状化した状態。溶けた物の様子を表すのによく使われる。
Expresses the texture of a smooth, almost liquefied material. The term is often used to describe something that is melted.

ゴクッ [*gokut*]：何かをのみ込む音。
Expresses the sound of gulping.

ホカホカ [*hoka hoka*]：暖かくて心地よい様子(類: ポカポカ)。
A synonym of *poka poka*. Describes a warm and comfortable situation.

料理・食べもの

食感①

① ― *Kukki no **saku saku** shita hazawari ga suki!*（I like the crispiness of cookies.）
― *Kocha nimo **pittari** ne.*（They go well with tea, too.）
② ― *Kono keki wa **shittori** shita shitazawari ne …*（This cake is moist.）
― ***Monyat** to shite ru wa.*（It's soft, too.）
③ ― *Kono senbei wa karai!*
（This rice cracker is hot!）
― ***Pirit** to shita ajitsuke da.*（It has a spicy seasoning.）
④ ***barit／bakit***
― *Sore ni katasugiru ne!*（It's too hard, as well!）

解説

サクサク ［*saku saku*］：歯ごたえの良さを表す（例：リンゴのサクサクした歯触り）。
Often used to describe crispiness or crunchiness. For example, *Ringo no saku saku shita hazawari.*（The crispy texture of an apple.）

ピッタリ ［*pittari*］：相性が合う様子、目的に合致する様子。
A perfect match.

シットリ ［*shittori*］：湿り気がある様子。心地よさや優雅さの含意がある。
Used to describe something moist, or a surface beaded with water. The expression indicates comfort and elegance.

モニャッ ［*monyat*］：食べ物が軟らかい様子。
A reference to foods that are soft.

ピリッ ［*pirit*］：辛さや痛みを表す。
Describes an impulsive reaction to spicy flavors or pain.

バリッ ［*barit*］：何かが割れる音、または強くかんで割る音。
Describes the sound of something being torn or bitten with force.

バキッ ［*bakit*］：何か厚いものが割れる音。「ポキッ」はそれより細いもの、または中が空洞のものが割れる音。
Describes the sound of something thick breaking. ***Pokit*** is used for the sound of something thin or hollow being broken.

Cooking & Food

食感②

[Panel 1] このモチモチした食感が好き…！

[Panel 2] フニャフニャして、私の好みじゃないわ…

[Panel 3] これはコリコリしてる / ほどよい歯ごたえね / シコシコ、シャキシャキしてる

① — Kono **mochi mochi** shita shokkan ga suki! (I like this chewiness.)
② — **Funya funya** shite, watashi no konomi ja nai wa … (This is too soft for my taste.)
③ — Kore wa **kori kori** shite iru. Hodoyoi hagotae ne. (This is crispy. It has a pleasant crunchiness.)
— **Shiko shiko**, **shaki shaki** shite ru. (It's firm and crispy.)

解説

モチモチ [*mochi mochi*]：餅から来た言葉で，柔らかく弾力性があり，粘り気のある様子(麺：モッチリ)。

The term comes from the texture of mochi, and therefore describes a soft, elastic and sticky texture. A synonym is *motchiri*.

フニャフニャ [*funya funya*]：マシュマロのように，とても柔らかい様子。

Describes a texture that is too soft and lacking in firmness, such as a marshmallow.

コリコリ [*kori kori*]：比較的固さのある物を噛んだときの音。典型例としては，中華料理のくらげが挙げられる。

The sound made when something relatively hard is chewed over and over again. Jellyfish—as prepared in Chinese cuisine—is a typical example of something that makes the sound of *kori kori* when chewed.

シコシコ [*shiko shiko*]：弾力性のある食べ物の心地よい歯ごたえを表す。

Describes the pleasant feeling of firm food.

シャキシャキ [*shaki shaki*]：野菜などのように歯ごたえのある食べ物の様子。セロリや大根が典型例。

Describes the crispy texture found in food like vegetables. Celery and daikon have the typical texture described by *shaki shaki*.

料理・食べもの

賞味期限

① **kun kun**
② — *Reizoko ni irete oitanoni, mo henna nioi ...!?*
　(Although I kept the dish in the refrigerator, it has already developed an odd smell.)
③ **poi**

解説

クンクン [*kun kun*]：においをかぐ様子。
Describes smelling something.

ポイ [*poi*]：深い考えもなしに何か捨てる，または放り投げる様子(例：たばこの吸い殻をポイと捨てる)。「ポイポイ」は程度や頻度が強まる。
Describes doing something without giving the action any thought. *Tabako no suigara o **poi** to suteru.* (He/she tosses out cigarette butts without a second thought.) ***Poi poi*** exaggerates the level or frequency of an act done with that feeling.

Cooking & Food

ひとくち

① *pero / kun kun*
② *pero*
　— *Hitokuchi dake ne ...* (You can only have one bite.)
③ *pero / taraa*
④ *gabut / mushat*

解説

ペロ [*pero*]：なめる様子，または舌を出す様子。
Refers to licking or sticking out one's tongue. ***Pero pero*** also refers to licking.

クンクン [*kun kun*]：においをかぐ様子。
Describes the act of smelling.

タラー（ッ） [*taraa(t)*]：何かが垂れ落ちる様子。ここではよだれが垂れる様子。
Refers to something dripping — in this case, the dog's drool.

ガブッ [*gabut*]：かみつく様子。
Describes biting into or swallowing something in one motion.

ムシャッ [*mushat*]：むさぼるように食べる様子，またはその音。
Describes the act or sound of eating voraciously. The term implies inelegance.

料理・食べもの

夏の食欲

解説

アッサリ [*assari*]：軽くて簡素な状態や味を表す。
Describes a condition or taste that is light or simple.

ギトギト [*gito gito*]：油っぽい様子。
Describes something oily.

ツルツル [*tsuru tsuru*]：口の中に入れたときに滑りが良い様子。
Describes a condition or texture that is slippery or smooth. Hiyamugi is a kind of noodle similar to udon, but much thinner. As hiyamugi is usually cooled with water right after being boiled and is dipped in a cold soup, it is a traditional summer favorite.

① — **Assari** shita mono ga tebetai na ... (I want to have something light.)
② — **Gito gito** shita mono wa shokuyoku ga wakanai ... (Oily food wouldn't make me feel like eating.)
③ — Hiyamugi nara doo? (How about hiyamugi cold noodles?)
 — Un, **tsuru tsuru** tto shita nodogoshi ga ii ne. (Oh, yes. I like their smooth, slurpable texture.)

Cooking & Food

おいしさのコツ

解説

サクサク [*saku saku*]：野菜など繊維の多い食材を切る音。クッキー，野菜，果物の歯触りを表すことも。
The sound of cutting fibrous foods, such as vegetables. The term also can indicate a pleasant texture for cookies, vegetables and fruit.

サッ [*sat*]：素早い動作を表す。
Describes doing something quickly.

ジャアー（ジャーッ） [*jaa (jaat)*]：物を炒める音。
The sound of food being stir-fried.

グツグツ [*gutsu gutsu*]：物が煮える音。
The sound of something boiling.

ジックリ [*jikkuri*]：何かを完了させるのに時間をかけること。
Describes taking time to complete something.

トロトロ [*toro toro*]：ゆるい火を表す。ほかに，粘度のある液体や，長い時間火が通されて原型をとどめないほど柔らかくなった食べ物を表す。
Refers to a very low flame. The term also describes viscous liquids, as well as ingredients that have become soft enough to lose their original shape after being cooked.

Panel 1: 野菜は小さく切って…　サクサク
Panel 2: 強火でサッと炒める　ジャアー
Panel 3: こちらはなべで煮込んでできあがりだ…　グツグツ
Panel 4: シチューは弱火でじっくり煮込むのよ…　トロトロだね

① — *Yasai wa chiisaku kitte …* (Cut the vegetables into small pieces …)
   saku saku
② — *Tsuyobi de **sat** to itameru.* (Fry them quickly on a high heat.)
   jaa
③ — *Kochira wa nabe de nikon de dekiagari da …* (Once this is boiled thoroughly, it'll be done.)
   gutsu gutsu
④ — *Shichu wa yowabi de **jikkuri** nikomu no yo …* (The stew should be boiled slowly on a low heat.)
   — ***Toro toro** da ne …* (Its texture looks just right.)

料理・食べもの

おいしさの表現

フワフワ [*fuwa fuwa*]：空気を含んで柔らかい様子。「フンワリ」は柔らかくて，ふっくらした様子が強調されている。
Describes a soft texture containing plenty of air. Its synonym, **funwari**, emphasizes a situation in which something is soft and puffed up.

ホクホク [*hoku hoku*]：イモやカボチャなどでんぷん質の食べ物が，十分加熱されていて心地よい歯触りである状態を表す。
Describes a favorable texture in which starchy foods, such as potatoes and pumpkins, are well cooked so that they are soft and can easily be split into pieces.

ホカホカ [*hoka hoka*]：柔らかくてふっくらした温かい物の様子。「湯上がりで体がホカホカしている」のようにも使う。
Describes a situation in which something warm is soft and puffed up. **Hoka hoka** can be used in a sentence like *Yuagari de karada ga hoka hoka shite iru* (My body feels warm after a bath).

① — **Fuwa fuwa** no pan ... （The bread is light and soft ...）
② — Kono yakiimo wa **hoku hoku** shite ru ...! （This baked sweet potato is soft and flaky.）
③ — **Hoka hoka** no gohan ... （This rice is nice and hot ...）

Cooking & Food

至福のひとくち

このチョコレートは 口に入れると トロ〜ッと溶けて…

①

香りが 口一杯に じわ〜っとひろがる…

②

③

> **解説**
>
> **トローッ**［*toroot*］：密度の濃い物がゆっくりと溶けてクリーム状になる様子。食べ物に関して使われる場合，美味の含意がある。「トロッ」や「トロリ」「トロトロ」も同義。
> Describes a highly concentrated object slowly melting to become a creamy consistency. When used for food, the term suggests deliciousness. ***Torot***, ***torori*** and ***toro toro*** are synonyms.
>
> **ジワーッ**［*jiwaat*］：少しずつ拡がる様子（類：ジワジワ）。
> Describes something that spreads or goes ahead steadily. ***Jiwa jiwa*** is a synonym.
>
> **シュルッ**［*shurut*］：ここでは，よだれをぬぐう音。
> Here, the term describes the sound of wiping away saliva.

① — *Kono chokoreto wa kuchi ni ireru to **toroot** to tokete …* (This chocolate should melt nicely as soon as I pop it into my mouth …)
② — *Kaori ga kuchi ippai ni **jiwaat** to hirogaru …* (And it gradually fills my whole mouth with a wonderful flavor …)
③ ***shurut***

料理・食べもの

麺料理

① **tsuru tsuru／suru suru**
— Kono men wa ... （These noodles ...）
② **mogu mogu**
— **Shiko shiko** shite iru ...!（...have an elastic texture.）
③ **zurut**
— Dashi jiru mo oishii ...!（The soup is tasty, too.）

解説

ツルツル [*tsuru tsuru*]：滑らかな食べ物をすする音。
The sound of slurping food with a smooth texture.

スルスル [*suru suru*]：何かが滑らかに動いたり進んだりする様子。ここでは，麺をすする音。
Describes something that is moving or progressing smoothly. In this situation, the term refers to the sound of slurping noodles.

モグモグ [*mogu mogu*]：食べ物をかむ音。
Describes the act of chewing food.

シコシコ [*shiko shiko*]：適度に硬く弾力があり心地よい歯ごたえを表す。
Suggests the pleasant chewy texture of some kinds of food.

ズルッ [*zurut*]：スープなど液状の食べ物をすする音。こうした行為は不作法と見なされかねないが，日本では美味であることを強調する表現として使われるときがある（類：ズズズ）。
The sound of slurping liquid food such as soup. This act may be regarded as a breach of manners, but in Japan the term is sometimes used to emphasize the delicious taste of a particular food. A synonym is *zu zu zu*.

Cooking & Food

ドッグフード

解説

ジッ [*jit*]：何かを見つめる様子。
Describes an act of staring at something.

ガサガサ [*gasa gasa*]：乾いているものがこすれたりする時の音。ここでは袋からドッグフードが出る音。
The sound of dry things rubbing against each other.
Here, it describes the dog food coming out of the package.

クンクン [*kun kun*]：においをかぐ様子。
Refers to an act of sniffing.

ムシャムシャ [*musha musha*]：ここでは, 犬が食べ物を口一杯にほおばって食べる様子。
In this case it indicates that the dog is stuffing its mouth with food.

ガツガツ [*gatsu gatsu*]：空腹から貪欲に食べる様子。
Describes eating greedily due to hunger.

ペロッ [*perot*]：素早く舌を出す様子や, 唇をなめる様子, あるいは一気に食べてしまう様子。
Refers to quickly sticking out one's tongue, the licking of lips or eating up something in one go.

① ***jit* / *gasa gasa***
　—*Mate!*（Wait.）
② ***kun kun***
③ ***musha musha* / *gatsu gatsu***
④ ***perot***

夏の飲み物

解説

グイッ [*guit*]：飲み物を勢いよく飲む音。ビールによく使う。
The sound of drinking fast—usually beer.

ゴクゴク [*goku goku*]：何かを勢いよく飲むときに喉が鳴る音。
The gulping sound made in the throat when drinking fast.

キリッ [*kirit*]：はっきりとした，辛口の味を表す。
Indicates a sharp, dry taste.

ゴクンゴクン [*gokun gokun*]：「ゴクゴク」と同義だが，飲み下す音がリズミカルに続く様子を表す。「ゴックンゴックン」はその強調形で，多量の飲み物が間隔を置いて飲み下される音を表す。
Similar to *goku goku*, but suggests the rhythmical sound of continuous drinking. *Gokkun gokkun* is its exaggerated form, suggesting big gulps separated by brief pauses.

① **guit / goku goku**
— Hieta biru ga umai kisetsu da（A cold beer tastes great at this time of year!）

② — Hieta koppuzake mo **kirit** to shite umai!（A cup of cold sake also has a nice sharp taste!）

③ **gokun gokun**
— Watashi wa suibun hokyu de natsu o norikiru!（I'll survive the summer by drinking plenty of water.）

Cooking & Food

食欲の秋

秋になると 何でも おいしく感じるわね‥
ムシャムシャ ①

ああ,何と幸せ!
パクパク モグモグ ②

秋は体重計を 無視する!
ヒョイ ③

解説

ムシャムシャ [*musha musha*]：口いっぱいに物を食べる様子。
Describes eating with a mouth full of food.

モグモグ [*mogu mogu*]：食べ物を噛んでいて口が動いている様子。
Describes a moving mouth to munch food.

パクパク [*paku paku*]：口を大きく開閉する動作を繰り返して物を食べる様子。
Refers to opening the mouth wide and closing it over and over again. It also describes eating food in such a way.

ヒョイ [*hyoi*]：軽やかにやすやすと体が動く様子。「ヒョイヒョイ」はこのような動作の反復を表す。
Refers to a body movement that appears light and easy. *Hyoi hyoi* suggests repeated movement of this kind.

① ***musha musha***
— *Aki ni naru to nandemo oishiku kanjiru wa nee …* (Everything seems to become delicious when autumn arrives, doesn't it?)

② ***mogu mogu／paku paku***
— *Aa, nanto shiawase!* (Oh, how happy I am!)

③ ***hyoi***
— *Aki wa taijukei o mushi suru!* (In autumn, I forget about the scales!)

ギョーザで元気

このお店のギョーザは皮が**パリッ**としておいしいのよ…

プ〜ンとしたニンニクの香りがいいね 具の風味も**バッチリ**だ！

モグモグ

ニンニク・パワーで元気**モリモリ**!!!

解説

パリッ [*parit*]：何かを割ったり，裂いたりする音。何かを噛む音にも使う。ここでは，薄くて歯ごたえの良いものを噛む音を表す。
The sound of splitting or ripping something. It also indicates the sound of biting. Here it is used to express the feel of biting into something thin and crispy.

モグモグ [*mogu mogu*]：ものを噛む様子。
Describes the movement of a mouth chewing something.

プーン [*puun*]：比較的強い匂いがする様子。
Describes a relatively strong smell.

バッチリ [*bacchiri*]：物事がうまくいっている様子，完璧な様子を表す。
Indicates that something is just right, or done perfectly.

モリモリ [*mori mori*]：新たな力がわく様子。
Indicates the gaining of new vigor or energy.

①— *Kono omise no gyoza wa kawa ga **parit** to site oishii no yo …* (This shop's gyoza are very tasty, as the skin is nice and crisp.)

② ***mogu mogu***
— ***Puun** to shita ninniku no kaori ga ii ne. Gu no fumi mo **bacchiri** da.* (There's a great smell of garlic. The filling also tastes wonderful.)

③— *Ninniku pawa de genki **mori mori**!* (The garlic has given me lots of energy!)

Cooking & Food

揚げ物

解説

パリパリ [*pari pari*]：軽くて，歯ごたえの良い様子。
Describes a light, crisp texture.

シナシナ [*shina shina*]：本来歯ごたえのあるべきものが，実際にはやわらかい様子。
Describes the soft texture of something that is supposed to be crispy.

モグモグ [*mogu mogu*]：食べ物を噛む様子。
Refers to food being chewed when the mouth is full.

サクッ [*sakut*]：軽くて歯ごたえの良い物を切ったり，砕いたり，あるいは割ったりする瞬間の音（類：サクサク）。
Describes the sound when something light, crisp and cool gets cut, crunched or broken apart with little resistance. *saku saku* is a synonym.

ギュウ [*gyuu*]：何かがきつく詰まっている様子。ここでは，女性の頭の中に料理の作り方がたくさん詰まっている様子を表す。
Indicates the compressing or tightening up of something. Here the term suggests the woman's brain is filled with a lot of cooking knowledge.

① — *Harumaki wa kawa ga **pari pari** shite oishii ne ...* (This spring roll with its crispy wrapper is delicious.)
　— *... Desho!* (It sure is!)

② — *Sameru to **shina shina** ni nattari suru kedo ...* (But they go soft when they get cold.)
　— *So naranai agekata aru no!* (There's a way of frying them that avoids that.)

③ **mogu mogu**
　— *Kono tempura mo koromo ga **sakut** to shita hazawari!* (This tempura batter also has a light, crispy texture.)
　— *Reshipi ga **gyuu** zume!* (My brain is packed full of recipes!)

料理・食べもの

かき氷

(speech bubbles in comic)
① かき氷はアイスクリームのようなベタベタした感じがないから好き
② シロップとよくかきまぜて…
③ 一度に大量にほうばるとノドと鼻がキーンとなる！！！

解説

ベタベタ [beta beta]：粘りつく様子（例：飴で手がベタベタする）。
Describes something sticky. For example, *Ame de te ga **beta beta** suru.* means "those sweets made my hands sticky."

ショリショリ [shori shori]：氷などが薄く削られる様子、またはその音。
Describes things like ice being crushed into fragments or the sound made when this happens.

サクサク [saku saku]：細かい粒や繊維質のものが、つぶされたり切られたりする様子、またはその音。
Used to describe small grains or fibrous items being cut or broken up, or the sound when this happens.

ウッ [ut]：うめき声。
A moan.

キーン [kiin]：耳や鼻、頭などを一瞬襲う鋭い痛み。
Indicates a sharp pain affecting the ears, nose or head for a split second.

ペロ [pero]：舌でなめる様子。
The sound of something being licked with a tongue, or that type of action.

① — *Karigori wa aisukurimu no yona **beta beta** shita kanji ga nai kara suki.*
(I prefer crushed ice to ice cream because it isn't sticky.)

② ***shori shori / saku saku***
— *Shiroppu to yoku kakimazete …*
(Mix well with syrup …)

③ — ***ut!***
— *Ichido ni tairyo ni hobaru to nodo to hana ga **kiin** to naru!* (But if you try to put a large amount in your mouth all at once, it'll hit you in the nose and throat!)

pero

Cooking & Food

晩酌

解説

チビリチビリ [*chibiri chibiri*]：類義語の「チビチビ」は物事を少しずつ行う様子。アルコールを飲む様子によく使う。「チビリチビリ」は，その動作の間が少し空くことを示唆している。
Its synonym, *chibi chibi*, indicates doing something over and over in small increments—often used to describe a way of drinking alcohol. *Chibiri chibiri* suggests pausing between sips.

グビグビ [*gubi gubi*]：液体を勢いよく飲む様子。
Gulping liquid.

グイグイ [*gui gui*]：グラスに入ったアルコールなどを力強く飲む様子。
Drinking in a dynamic or vigorous manner, such as when drinking shots of liquor.

① *chibiri chibiri*
② *gubi gubi*
— *Koppuzake ni shiyo ...* （I'll switch to pull-tab cup sake.）
③ — *Kono sake wa **gui gui** ikeso da ...* （This sake makes me want to drink a lot.）

かくし味

① **dosat**
— Tsuyobi de **sat** to itameru dake …! (It's OK to just stir-fry them.)
② **jaat**
③ **juut**
— Kakushiaji ni biru o **choppiri** …! Ki ga tsukanai daro … (I just add a little beer for some hidden flavor. I don't think they'll notice.)

ドサッ [*dosat*]：大きなものが一つ，あるいは小さなものがまとまって落下する様子，またはその音。ここではフライパンの中に食材が放り込まれる様子。
Describes a situation in which one large item or a number of small items are dropped suddenly and the sound generated in such a scenario. In this case, the term refers to many ingredients being thrown into a frying pan.

サッ [*sat*]：軽い，瞬間的な動作を表す。
Describes a light movement or action that is made in a moment.

ジャーッ [*jaat*]：食べ物を強火で炒める時の音。
When frying food over a high flame.

ジューッ [*juut*]：液体や何か湿った物の水分が，熱いものとの接触で急に蒸発する音。食べ物を炒めるときの音によく使われる。英語の「sizzle」にあたる。
Describes the sound of juice evaporating suddenly when a liquid or something moist comes into contact with something hot. The term is often used when frying food and corresponds to "sizzle."

チョッピリ [*choppiri*]：少量を表す。
Refers to a small amount.

Chapter 4

Feelings & Emotions
気持ち・感情

| Feelings & Emotions

笑い①

① *kat kat ka*
② *ki ki ki*
③ *ku ku ku*
④ *keta keta / geta geta / gera gera*

解説

カッカッカ [*kat kat ka*]：短い音のつながりで，男らしい笑い方を表す。ただし，優雅な笑い方ではない。
This succession of short sounds is meant to communicate a hearty, manly laugh, but it is not considered elegant.

キキキ [*ki ki ki*]：ヒステリックな笑い。
Hysterical laughter.

ククク [*ku ku ku*]：忍び笑い。
A giggle.

ケタケタ [*keta keta*]：品がなく，ややヒステリックな甲高い笑い。
A vulgar laugh in a slightly hysterical, high-pitched tone.

ゲタゲタ [*geta geta*]：大口を開けて品なく笑うさま。
A vulgar laugh.

ゲラゲラ [*gera gera*]：ゲタゲタと同様。「ゲタゲタ」は単に声のトーンを表すこともあるが，「ゲラゲラ」は体全体で笑っている様子を表す。
While *geta geta* tends to indicate only the tone of voice, this expression gives the impression that the entire body is shaking with laughter.

｜ 気持ち・感情

笑い②

① a ha ha ／ a hha hha
② i hi hi ／ i hhi hhi
③ u hu hu ／ u hhu hhu
④ e he he ／ e hhe hhe
⑤ o ho ho ／ o hho hho

解説

アハハ [*a ha ha*]：無邪気な笑い。
　The sound of innocent laughter.
アッハッハッ [*a hha hha*]：にぎやかな笑い声(類: ワッハッハ)。
　The sound of uproarious laughter. Its synonyms is ***wa hha hha***.
イヒヒ [*i hi hi*]：悪意のある笑い。相手をからかったりバカにしたりするときの笑いを表すことも。
　The sound of spiteful laughter. It is the kind of laughter used when making fun of or mocking others.
イッヒッヒ [*i hhi hhi*]：意地の悪そうな笑い。
　The sound of malicious laughter.
ウフフ [*u hu hu*]：おかしさ，うれしさなどで思わずもらす笑い声。
　The sound of light laughter uttered unconsciously with amusement or joy.
ウッフッフッ [*u hhu hhu*]：ウフフと同義。
　A synonym for ***u hu hu***.
エヘヘ [*e he he*]：控えめな笑い声。
　The sound of modest laughter.
エッヘッヘッ [*e hhe hhe*]：心からの，自信に満ちた笑い。
　The sound of a hearty, confident laugh.
オホホ [*o ho ho*]：女性の上品な笑い声。
　The sound of an elegant woman's laugh.
オッホッホ [*o hho hho*]：女性の気取った笑い声。
　The sound of a pretentious woman's laugh.

Feelings & Emotions

なき声

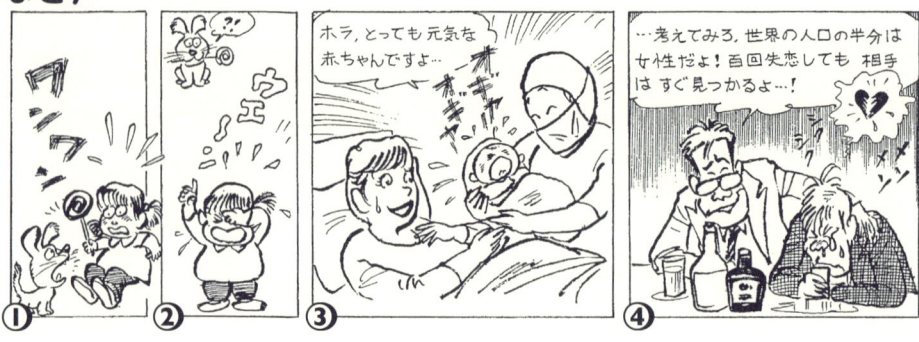

① **wan wan**
② **ueen**
③ **ogyaa ogyaa**
  — Hora, tottemo genki na akachan desu yo.（Look, you have a very healthy baby.）
④ **shiku shiku／meso meso**
  — Kangaetemiro. Sekai no jinko no hanbun wa josei da yo. Hyakkai shitsuren shite mo, aite wa sugu mitsukaru yo.（Think about this. Women make up half of the world's population. So even if you are dumped 100 times, you will eventually find a new partner.）

解説

ワンワン [*wan wan*]：犬がほえる声。猫の鳴き声は「ニャー」。
　The sound of a dog's bark. The sound of a cat's meow is ***nyaaa***.

ウェーン [*ueen*]：子どもが口を大きく開けて泣く声。
　The sound of a frustrated or disappointed child crying with his or her mouth wide open.

オギャー　オギャー [*ogyaa ogyaa*]：新生児の泣き声。
　The sound a newborn baby makes when it cries.

シクシク [*shiku shiku*]：静かに泣く様子。
　Sobbing or weeping quietly.

メソメソ [*meso meso*]：弱々しく泣く様子。
　Synonym of ***shiku shiku***. Whimpering.

お説教

① *gami gami* ／ *kote kote* ／ *nechi nechi*
② *muka muka*
— Anmari **kudo kudo** iu na. Imadoki no wakamono wa kireyasui kara. (Don't grumble so much. Young people nowadays lose their tempers so easily.)
③ *mukaa* ／ *wana wana*
— **Puttsun** ga kowai. Osekkyo mo **hodo hodo** ni shinakya. (It's scary when they suddenly losing their tempers. We'd better keep our lecturing to a minimum.)

解説

ガミガミ [*gami gami*]：かみつくように言う様子。他人をしかりつけるときに使う。
Snappishly. Used when a person blows up at another.

コテコテ [*kote kote*]：何かが過度にある様子。関西地方で特に一般的。
Used when referring to something being excessive; this phrase is particularly common in the Kansai region.

ネチネチ [*nechi nechi*]：粘ついたり，しつこかったりする様子。
Sticky or stubbornly tenacious.

ムカムカ [*muka muka*]：吐き気を催すような気持ち。ここでは強いいら立ち，怒りを表す。
When one feels like throwing up. Here, it describes irritation or anger.

クドクド [*kudo kudo*]：長時間にわたって話すこと。長々と話すこと。
Talking at great length; dwelling on a subject.

ムカアァ（ムカーッ） [*mukaa (t)*]：強い怒りがこみ上げる様子。
Disgusted.

ワナワナ [*wana wana*]：怒りで震えること。
Trembling with anger.

プッツン [*puttsun*]：ひもなどが急に切れる時の様子やその音。怒りで感情を爆発させる様子を表現する。最近では「キレる」がよく使われる。
Describes the sound or state of a piece of string or something similar suddenly breaking. The term is used when a person explodes in rage. Recently, the word *kireru* is often used to describe the same state.

悲しみ

① **gakkuri**
— Petto ga **pokkuri** shindanda... Boku no jinsei ni **pokkari** ana ga aita mitai.（My pet died. Its death left an empty space in my heart.）
② **gushu**
— Nani o katteta no?（What kind of pet did you have?）
③ — Gokiburi!（A cockroach!）
dota

ガックリ [*gakkuri*]：ひどく落ち込んでいること。
State of big disappointment.

ポックリ [*pokkuri*]：何かが途中でもろく折れる様子。ここでは突然の死を表す。
Describes something fragile snapping easily. Here it describes a sudden death.

ポッカリ [*pokkari*]：丸い穴が空いている状態を表し、「ポカリ」の強調形。
Pokkari describes a circular hole that is open. It is a stressed form of *pokari*.

グシュ [*gushu*]：すすり泣く様子やその音。
State or sound of sobbing.

ドタ [*dota*]：何かが倒れた時の音。驚きを大げさに見せるためにひっくり返る様子。ここでは、友達のペットがゴキブリだったことに驚いたのを強調している。
The sound of something falling. It is common to show exaggerated surprise by falling over. In this cartoon, the boy is exaggerating his surprise at his friend's choice of pet.

孤独

① *potsun*
② *porot*
③ *shun*

ポツン [*potsun*]：孤独だったり，他の人から引き離されている状態を表す。
Refers to loneliness or the state of being set apart from others.

ポロッ [*porot*]：小さい物(ここでは涙)が落ちる様子を表す。「ホロっと／ホロリとする」はそのような時の感傷的な気持ちを表すのに使われる。
Describes something small falling off something else: in this case, tears. ***Horot to/ horori to suru*** is used to describe a sentimental feeling in such a case.

シュン [*shun*]：意気消沈する様子。
Expresses the feeling of dejection.

小言はほどほどに

解説

キンキン [*kin kin*]：金属的な音。ここでは高い、ヒステリックな声を表す。
A metallic sound used here to describe a high-pitched hysterical voice.

ブツブツ [*butsu butsu*]：不同意なことや不満を小声で言う様子。
Describes murmuring discontent and dissatisfaction.

ガミガミ [*gami gami*]：やかましく文句を言う様子。
Refers to a person snapping at another.

ポンポン [*pon pon*]：遠慮なく言葉が次から次に出てくる様子。
Suggests a situation in which someone is saying words one after another without reserve.

プリプリ [*puri puri*]：人が怒っている様子。
Indicates that someone is angry.

① — ！
② — **Kin kin** *koe o hariage naku te mo...*（You don't have to scream at me at the top of your voice.）
　butsu butsu
③ — *Itsumo* **gami gami** *urusai yo...*（You're always snapping at me.）
④ **pon pon** / **puri puri**
　— *Tsukiatte orenai yo...*（I can't get along with them.）

プレゼント

①**doki doki**
　— Amerika no tomodachi kara kozutsumi da. Nan daro?（A parcel from one of my friends in the United States? I wonder what it is?）
②**poi poi ／ gasa goso ／ waku waku**
③**jaaan**
　— Matsui-senshu no sain boru da!（It's a ball autographed by major league baseball player Hideki Matsui!）

解説

ドキドキ [*doki doki*]：心臓が鼓動する音。類義語の「ワクワク」と一緒に使われることが多い。
The sound of a heart beating. Often used together with its synonym *waku waku*.

ポイポイ [*poi poi*]：何かを軽く投げる様子。
Describes an act of tossing something.

ガサゴソ [*gasa goso*]：紙や葉などの物がこすれて摩擦する音や様子。
Describes objects such as paper and leaves rubbing against each other.

ワクワク [*waku waku*]：何かいいことが起きることを期待して興奮している気持ちを表す。
Describes a feeling of excitement in anticipation of something nice.

ジャーン [*jaaan*]：ここでは野球ボールが驚きだったことを表すのに使われている。誰かを驚かそうとしている人は，予期せぬことを起こそうとしている時に注意を引き付けるためにこの表現が使える。
Here the term indicates the item is a surprise or unexpected. Those who try to surprise someone may use the expression to draw attention when they are about to produce something unexpected.

Feelings & Emotions

気持ちも空も

①就職が決まらずブラブラしてるよ…

②気分は梅雨空だね… どんより

③気持ちも空も早くパァーッと明るくなりたいね！

解説

ブラブラ [*bura bura*]：何かが他の物から垂れ下がって揺れていること。あるいは，安定しているべき物が不安定な様子で揺れ動いていること。特に何もせず時間を過ごす様子を表すこともある。

Describes an object dangling off something else and wavering, or something that should be stable swinging in an unstable way. The term also can be used to describe loitering or spending time without doing much.

ドンヨリ [*donyori*]：空や気持ち，表情などが重くて暗い様子。

Describes a dark and heavy sky, feeling or facial expression.

パァーッ [*paat*]：何かが一瞬で消えたり広がったりすること。ここでは，重苦しいことがすぐになくなってほしいという発言者の希望を表す。

Describes something instantly disappearing or spreading. In this case, it indicates the speaker's hope that all the gloominess would just instantly go away.

シラー [*shiraa*]：陰気な気持ちや雰囲気を表す。

Describes a cheerless feeling or atmosphere.

① — *Shushoku ga kimarazu **bura bura** shiteru yo...* (I'm just hanging around doing nothing because I can't find a job.)

② ***donyori***
 — *Kibun wa tsuyu zora da ne...* (I feel glum, like these rainy season clouds.)

③ — *Kimochi mo sora mo hayaku **paat** to akaruku naritai ne...!* (Hopefully, both your mood and the sky will clear up soon!)
 shiraa

警戒中

解説

ジロッ [*jirot*]：他人に向けた，鋭く責めるような視線。類義語「ジロリ」はより長い時間見つめていることで，「ジローッ」は凝視している様子。「ジロジロ」は好奇心や疑いの気持ちでしつこく見つめる様子。

Describes a sharp, accusing glance made at someone else. Its synonym, *jirori*, indicates a longer glance, while *jiroot* indicates staring. *Jiro jiro* suggests glancing at something insistently, often out of curiosity or suspicion.

ピリピリ [*piri piri*]：とても神経質になっている様子。

Indicates someone getting very nervous.

ノホホン [*nohohon*]：無邪気で気楽な様子。

Describes naive and nonchalant attitude.

① *jirot*
② — Tero taisaku de machi no funiki ga **piri piri** shiteru ne... (The whole city's on edge because of efforts that have been made to prevent terrorist attacks.)
③ — **Nohohon** to shite ita jidai ga natsukashii...! (I miss the days when things were more relaxed...)

Feelings & Emotions

失恋

①**butsu butsu**
— **Mogo mogo** iwanai de **zubat** to itte miro!（Don't mutter, speak clearly!）
②**gakkuri**
— Ichido ya nido no shitsuren de **uji uji** suru na. **Meso meso** surun ja nai!
(Don't get all sulky over a heartbreak or two. You don't need to sob your heart out.)
③**dosat**
— Chikyujo ni dokushinjosei ga nanokunin iru ka shirabete miro!（Try finding out how many millions of single women are in the world!）

ブツブツ [*butsu butsu*]：小声で言うさま。
Describes grumbling under one's breath.
モゴモゴ [*mogo mogo*]：口を大きく開けずにしゃべる様子。
Mumbling in an unclear voice.
ズバッ [*zubat*]：物事の核心に明確にまっすぐ向かうさま。
Used when being clear, straightforward and going right to the heart of the matter.
ガックリ [*gakkuri*]：失望している様子。
Describes disappointment.
ウジウジ [*uji uji*]：煮え切らず内向きになって物事の決断が出来なくなっている様子。「イジイジ」も同様の使い方をするが，臆病な性格も表す。
Indicates that someone has become very hesitant and introverted and can no longer make a decision. *Iji iji* can be used in a similar way but also suggests a timid character.
メソメソ [*meso meso*]：すすり泣くさま。
Describes whimpering, whining.
ドサッ [*dosat*]：比較的大量の物や大きな物が一気に落とされたり投げ出されたりするさま。またはそのような時に発生する音。ここでは上司が人口についての本一式を投げ出している。
Describes a relatively large amount of something or relatively large objects falling down or being thrown down at the same time, as well as the sound made by such an occurrence. In this case, the boss throws down a pile of books on population statistics.

挑戦

ワクワク [*waku waku*]：期待することがあって興奮している様子を表す。類義語「ドキドキ」はそのような状況での心臓の鼓動に焦点を置いている。
Describes a feeling of being excited with anticipation. Its synonym, **doki doki**, puts emphasis on one's heartbeat in such a situation.

イライラ [*ira ira*]：ストレスを感じたり，いらだたしい時に使われる。
Used when someone suffers stress or feels frustrated.

ムッ [*mut*]：不機嫌，不愉快になる時使われる。
Used when someone gets pouty and displeased.

① **waku waku**
— *Osomaki nagara pasokonyuza no nakama ni naru zo.* (Though I'm doing it a little late, I'm becoming a computer user like everyone else!)

② **ira ira**
— *Setsumeisho o yonde mo yogo no imi ga wakaran...* (Even though I read the instruction book, I still have no idea what the technical terms mean.)

③ **mut**
— *Ekimae no pasokon sukuru ni kayottara doo?* (How about going to the computer school by the station?)
— *Jugyoryo wa yoso gai da!* (Tuition for such a school is an unexpected expense!)

Feelings & Emotions

テレビドラマ

(Comic panel 1) このドラマは、いつも**ハラハラ ドキドキ**させるね…

(Comic panel 2) 胸が**キュン**となって… 感動が**ひたひたと**伝わってくる…

(Comic panel 3)

① — *Kono dorama wa itsumo **hara hara doki doki** saseru ne…* (This drama always makes me excited.)

② — *Mune ga **kyun** to natte…* (It makes your heart twinge…)
 — *Kando ga **hita hita** to tsutawatte kuru…* (Your emotions build up inside of you gradually.)

③ ***gushu / horot***

解説

ハラハラ [*hara hara*]：気がかりなことがあったり，危険を感じたりして不安な気持ちになる様子。
Describes the state of being anxious due to some concern or sense of danger.

ドキドキ [*doki doki*]：恐怖や興奮で心臓が鼓動すること。
Refers to a heart that is beating fast due to fear or excitement.

キュン [*kyun*]：同情や感動で胸が締め付けられるさま。
Typically describes a heart twinging with sympathy or emotion.

ヒタヒタ [*hita hita*]：水面のような平らなものが他のものに軽く打ち付ける小さな動きを表す。またはそのような時に発生する音。比ゆ的に何かが少しずつ近付いて来る様子も表す。
Describes a small movement of something flat—like the surface of water—that hits lightly against something else, or the sound made from such a movement. Metaphorically, the term also suggests something coming closer little by little.

グシュ [*gushu*]：ここでは泣いて鼻をかむ音。
The sound made when blowing one's nose.

ホロッ [*horot*]：心を動かす出来事に対して涙が突然ほおを伝わるさま。
Describes the moment when tears suddenly start rolling down a person's cheeks, usually because of some moving or inspiring event.

気持ち・感情

親の気持ち

解説

バアー [*baa*]：赤ちゃんと遊んだり，隠した顔や表情を突然見せたりする時に使われる。
The word used when playing with a baby or suddenly revealing a hidden face or facial expression.

キョトン [*kyoton*]：予期しなかったり事情が飲み込めなかったりして，困惑や驚きで目を見開いてぼんやりしたさま。
A wide-eyed, dazed expression of confusion and surprise in response to something unexpected or difficult to understand.

ニコニコ [*niko niko*]：笑っている顔。
Describes a smiling face.

ハラハラ [*hara hara*]：→ see page 92.

ドキドキ [*doki doki*]：→ see page 92.

ワクワク [*waku waku*]：何かいいことが起こることを期待して興奮すること。
Indicates excitement in anticipation of something good.

ヒヤヒヤ [*hiya hiya*]：「ハラハラ」の類義語。恐れや不安を抱いているようす。
A synonym of *hara hara*. Expresses fear or anxiety.

① — **Baa! Kyoton** to shiteru...!（Peekaboo! She looks a bit surprised.）
② **niko niko**
　— A, waratta!（Oh, she smiled.）
③ — Kono ko ga seijin shite jiritsu suru made, oya wa **hara hara, doki doki, waku waku, hiya hiya** no renzoku ni nariso ne...（Until she becomes an adult and independent, her parents will have a constant stream of anxiety, thrills, excitement and worries.）
　— Sore ga oya no ikigai ni naru no yo...（For parents, that'll make life worthwhile.）

怒り

スゴスゴ [*sugo sugo*]：気落ちや失望したままその場所を去って行くさま。
Describes someone as they leave a particular place in dejection or disappointment.

ペコペコ [*peko peko*]：お辞儀を何度も繰り返す卑屈な行動を表す。
Describes the subservient act of bowing, over and over.

ムカムカ [*muka muka*]：気分が悪い時の吐き気。ここでは怒りが込み上げて来るさま。
Refers to a nauseous feeling when you are sick. In this case, the term describes a surge of anger.

カンカン [*kan kan*]：強い怒りで興奮しているさま。
Describes a raging anger.

① — Ikkatsu sarete **sugo sugo** hikisagattari... (Dejectedly caving in if you're scolded even once...)

② **muka muka**
— **Peko peko** to iinari ni naru yatsu wa kirai da... (... Always bowing and doing just as others say — I hate guys who act like that!)

③ — **Kan kan** ni okotteru ne... yare yare... (He really flies off the handle. Good grief ...)

気持ち・感情

やる気まんまん

モリモリ [*mori mori*]：やる気やエネルギーがありあまるさま。
Describes when someone is filled with motivation or energy.

キリリ [*kiriri*]：気を引き締めること。または、物をしっかり締めること。ここでは鉢巻きを締めて気を引き締めている。
Describes bracing for a challenge—in this case, the man is doing so by tying a band around his head—or tightening something up.

バリバリ [*bari bari*]：精力的に仕事をすること。
Refers to working energetically.

バンバン [*ban ban*]：強い力で、一気に、あるいは立て続けに何かをこなすこと。
Suggests doing something with great force, in large quantity or in a row.

ドンドン [*don don*]：加速度的に何かが進んでいるさま。
Indicates something is progressing at an accelerated rate.

①—**Mori mori** iyoku ga waite kita!（I've become more and more motivated.）
kiriri

②—**Bari bari** shigoto o suru zo! **Ban ban** katazuke te yaru!!（I'll work super hard! I'll get it done lickity-split!!）

③—**Don don** shigoto o motte koi!（Bring on the work!）

Feelings & Emotions

いい陽気

ポカポカ [*poka poka*]：適度に暖かいさま。快適な感じを意味することが多い。
Suggests being moderately warm, usually indicating being comfortable.

ブラッ [*burat*]：特に目的もなく行動を起こす様子。ここでは散策すること(類：ブラブラ)。
Describes a situation when someone takes action without a specific purpose—in this case, wandering around. *Bura bura* is a synonym.

ウキウキ [*uki uki*]：何かいいことを体験したり期待したりする時に感じる幸せな、またはうれしい気持ちを表す。類義語は「ルンルン」。「ワクワク」と一緒に使われることが多いが、「ワクワク」はいいことを期待する時の興奮した気持ちに力点がある。
Suggests that someone has a happy or pleasant feeling when experiencing or expecting something good. *Run run* is a synonym. *Uki uki* is often used with *waku waku* as a set phrase, but *waku waku* puts more emphasis on the excitement of expecting something good to happen.

① — **Poka poka** yoki da... (It's warm and pleasant.)
② — **Burat** to sanpo shite kibun tenkan. (I'll wander around and recharge my batteries.)
③ **uki uki**

気持ち・感情

不平不満

解説

ブツブツ [*butsu butsu*]：小声でつぶやくさま。
Describes murmuring.

ペコペコ [*peko peko*]：何度も頭を下げる様子。大抵，こびへつらったりおだてたりする態度を表す。
Refers to bowing over and over—usually in an obsequious or flattering manner.

ムカッ [*mukat*]：比ゆ的に，怒りで吐き気を感じるさま。動詞形では「ムカムカする」。よりくだけた表現に「ムカツク」がある。
By extension, the term is used to describe feeling a surge of anger to the point of nausea. Its verb form is *muka muka suru*. *Mukatsuku* is its casual variation.

ビリビリ [*biri biri*]：布や紙など薄い物を破る時の音。そういった行動も表す。
The sounds made when ripping thin materials, such as clothes and paper. Also refers to such an action.

① ***butsu butsu***
— *Kurai nyusu ga oosugiru!* (There's too much gloomy news!)
② — ***Peko peko*** *atama o sagete sumu koto de wa nai!* (Merely bowing over and over doesn't make things better!)
mukat
③ ***biri biri***
— *Takarakuji mo ataranai shi...!* (To make matters worse, I didn't win the lottery.)

| Feelings & Emotions

待ち合わせ

解説

ソワソワ [*sowa sowa*]：期待や興奮，心配事のために落ち着かない態度や感情を表す。
Indicates a restless attitude or feeling due to anticipation, excitement or worry.

イライラ [*ira ira*]：欲求不満やいらだち，神経過敏などの不快な気持ちを表す。
Indicates one is experiencing an uncomfortable feeling such as frustration, irritation or nerves.

キョロキョロ [*kyoro kyoro*]：落ち着かない様子で周りを見回す行動。
Describes the act of looking around in a restless manner.

ホッ [*hot*]：安堵の溜め息をもらすこと。重圧やストレス，責任から解放され安心した気持ちも表す。
Describes the act of letting out a sigh of relief. It also indicates that one feels relieved when freed from pressure, stress or responsibility.

①*sowa sowa*
②*ira ira* ／ *kyoro kyoro*
　— *Osoi naa...*（She's late.）
③*hot*
　— *Kita!*（She's here!）

議論白熱

① wai wai / kari kari / jiri jiri
② waa waa / gami gami
③ pit / pat
　—Urusai!（Shut up!）

解説

ワイワイ [*wai wai*]：大勢の人がにぎやかに騒いでいる様子や，そのような場面の音を表す。類義語の「ガヤガヤ」はそういった音を全体的に表し，不愉快な気持ちが含まれている。
Describes many people speaking loudly, or the sounds made in such a situation. Its close synonym, *gaya gaya*, treats the combined sounds as a whole and indicates an uncomfortable feeling toward such noise.

カリカリ [*kari kari*]：神経質になったり，いらだっているさま。
Indicates someone is getting nervous and irritated.

ジリジリ [*jiri jiri*]：もどかしくていらだっているさま。
Indicates someone feeling frustrated.

ワアワア [*waa waa*]：「ワイワイ」の類義語。大声を出している様子。
Synonym of *wai wai*. Speaking loudly.

ガミガミ [*gami gami*]：やかましく文句を言う様子。
Describes a person snapping at another.

ピッ [*pit*]：笛の音やリモコンのボタンを押した時などの短く高い音を表す。
Describes a short, high-pitched noise, such as a whistle or the sound of pushing a button on a remote control.

パッ [*pat*]：行動や状態が突然変化すること。ここではテレビが消えた様子。
Refers to a sudden change in behavior or condition. In this case, the television has been turned off.

Chapter 5

Conditions & Health
体調・健康

Conditions & Health

飲みすぎに注意

① — *Doshita no?* (What's wrong?)
— *I ga **muka muka**, **chiku chiku** surunda...* (I fell like throwing up and I have a prickly pain in my stomach.)
② — *Atama ga omokute, **zuki zuki** suru...!* (My head feels really heavy and I feel a throbbing pain.)
— *Futsukayoi daro. Shibaraku **boot** to shitereba naoru sa.* (Must be a hangover. If you just do nothing for a while, you'll feel better.)
③ —*Kizu ga **zuki zuki** suru.* (I have a bruise that is throbbing.)
— *Sakuya, yotte koronda toki no kizu daro?* (You must have got it last night when you got drunk and fell down.)

ムカムカ [*muka muka*]：吐き気を催している状態。
Muka muka refers to a feeling of nausea.
チクチク [*chiku chiku*]：針で刺されるような痛みを表す。
Chiku chiku describes a prickly pain.
ズキズキ [*zuki zuki*]：脈打つように痛むこと。
Describes a sudden, throbbing pain.
ボーッ [*boot*]：何もしないで過ごす様子。
Describes the state of doing nothing.

視力検査

① *jit* ／ *pitat* ／ *boyaat*

> **ジッ** ［*jit*］：一心に見つめる様子。
> Describes the state of looking at something intently.
> **ピタッ** ［*pitat*］：ものが他の何かに貼りついている様子や，突然動きや音が止まることを表す。
> Describes sticking one thing to another or suddenly stopping something. *Kare wa tabako o **pittat** to yameta.* (He stopped smoking altogether.)
> **ボヤーッ** ［*boyaat*］：輪郭があいまいな様子。「ボーッ（と）」「ボケーッ」「ボンヤリ」も同様の意味。不明瞭な様子を指す。
> Refers to vague outlines. Its synonyms are ***boot to,*** ***bokeet*** and ***bonyari***. It also describes things that are visibly unclear.

Conditions & Health

花粉症

解説

ポロポロ [*poro poro*]：小さいものが粒状のかたまりになって落ちる様子。
Describes something crumbling down.

ムズムズ [*muzu muzu*]：虫が体の上を動いている時に起きるような、くすぐったい感覚。ここでは，鼻の粘膜が花粉のせいでかゆい様子を表している。
Indicates a tickling sensation that feels like it is caused by the movement of a tiny insect. In this case, the term describes the itchy feeling of nasal membranes reacting to the presence of pollen.

ハックショーン [*hakkushoon*]：大きなクシャミの音を表す日本語の典型的表現。
A typical sound in Japanese for a big sneeze.

① — *Namida ga* **poro poro** *tomaranai shi...* （I can't stop crying...）
② — *Hana wa* **muzu muzu** *suru shi...* （I feel an itch inside my nose...）
③ ***hakkushoon***
 — *Kafunsho no kisetsu wa tsurai ne...* （The hay fever season is terrible, isn't it?）

胃の健康

ゴロゴロ [*goro goro*]：大きなものが転がる様子や，そのことで生じる音を指す。ここでは，お腹の調子が悪いときの音や様子。
Describes heavy objects rolling or the sound such an action makes. In this case, it describes the sound coming from an upset stomach.

チクチク [*chiku chiku*]：針のようなもので刺されたような感覚。
Describes a feeling as if being pricked by a needlelike object.

キリキリ [*kiri kiri*]：錐状のもので刺されたかのような痛み。
Describes pain as if being stabbed by a big needle.

ムカムカ [*muka muka*]：吐き気がする様子。
Indicates a feeling as if one wants to vomit.

① — Onaka ga **goro goro** shitari... (My stomach keeps rumbling...)
② — **Chiku chiku** shitari...**kiri kiri** tto nattari... (Sometimes it hurts briefly, but sometimes I feel a sharp pain...)
③ — **Muka muka** shitari... (I feel nauseous...)
— Kuwashiku mite mimasho... (Let's take a closer look.)

Conditions & Health

長生きの秘訣

解説

ヨボヨボ [*yobo yobo*]：高齢のせいで肉体的にすっかり衰えている人の様子。
Describes someone who is physically weak due to old age.

ヨタヨタ [*yota yota*]：足取りがおぼつかない様子。「ヨチヨチ」は，幼児のぎこちない歩き方を指す表現。
Refers to an unsteady gait. *Yochi yochi* is used to describe toddlers walking in a similar manner.

シャン [*shan*]：緊張した気持ちや態度を表す(類: ピン)。
Describes a tense feeling or attitude. *Pin* is its synonym.

ヨレヨレ [*yore yore*]：元の形状を失ってしまい，シワができたりみすぼらしくなった状態を指す。
Refers to something that has lost its original shape, resulting in wrinkles or shabbiness.

ピンピン [*pin pin*]：元気あふれる人や健康な人の様子。
Describes someone who is cheerful and in good health.

ハハハ [*ha ha ha*]：温和な笑い声。
Warm laughter.

① — *Yaa, ogenki desu ka?* (Hi, how are you?)
— *Konnichiwa.* (Hello.)
yobo yobo／yota yota

② — *Itsumo sesuji ga **shan** to shite imasu ne...* (Your posture is always so straight.)

③ — *Watashi wa, karada wa **yore yore** demo kimochi dake wa **pin pin** shite imasu!* (My body might be getting old, but I still feel young inside!)
ha ha ha
— *Nagaiki no hiketsu desu ne...* (That must be the key to longevity.)

風邪

のどが **ムズムズ** するんだ…

①

ぼくは のどが **ヒリヒリ** するので うがいをしてる…

②

気分が **パッ** としないね…

コホン

③

解説

ムズムズ [*muzu muzu*]：皮膚の上や鼻の中や喉において，小さな虫が這うような不愉快な感覚。
Describes an uncomfortable feeling like tiny insects crawling over the skin, nasal passages or throat.

ヒリヒリ [*hiri hiri*]：皮膚や粘膜の表面が持続して刺激を受けて痛む感覚。
Describes a stinging sensation that feels like the skin or mucous membrane is repeatedly pricked.

パッ [*pat*]：瞬間的に起きる行動や現象，または変化を指す。ひいては，派手で華々しい様子を指す。「パッとしない」は，つまらない，地味な様子のこと。
Describes an action, phenomenon or a change that takes place in an instant. By extension, the term is also used to describe something flashy and spectacular. Therefore, **pat to shinai** refers to something dull and unspectacular.

コホン [*kohon*]：小さな咳の音。
The sound of a small cough.

①— Nodo ga **muzu muzu** surun da... (I have a tickle in my throat.)
②— Boku wa nodo ga **hiri hiri** suru no de ugai o shiteru... (My throat is so sore I've been gargling.)
③— Kibun ga **pat** to shinai ne... (Feeling like this, it's hard to feel well, isn't it?)
kohon

こたつ

① *kokkuri kokkuri*
② *goron* / *uto uto*
— *Aa nemui...* (Ahh, I'm sleepy...)
③ *munya munya*
— *Utatane wa kaze o hikimasu yo...* (You'll catch a cold if you have a catnap.)

コックリコックリ [*kokkuri kokkuri*]：「コックリ」は基本的に，頭を上げ下げする動き，つまり，うなずきを指す。「コックリコックリ」は，体を起こした状態で頭を上下にふらつかせながら眠る人の様子。

Kokkuri alone basically refers to the action of moving the head up and down — i.e. nodding. Repeated twice, *kokkuri kokkuri* describes the rising and falling head of a person who is sleeping while sitting up.

ゴロン [*goron*]：無造作に横になって寝る時の表現。

Describes someone lying down gently.

ウトウト [*uto uto*]：うたた寝するような眠気。「ウツラウツラ」も同じような眠りを表すのに使う。

Describes feeling sleepy enough to have a short nap. *Utsura utsura* can be also used for a similar sleep.

ムニャムニャ [*munya munya*]：何を言っているのか聞き取れないような寝言を言っている様子。

Refers to muttering that is not understandable.

体調・健康

育て方

スクスク育って、また大きくなったわネ！

クリクリした目が とても かわいい！

ノビノビ 育てようと思っています。アクセクしてもねえ…！

解説

スクスク [*suku suku*]：子どもや動物、植物が、何の問題もなく早く成長する様子。
Describes young children, animals or plants growing quickly without problems.

クリクリ [*kuri kuri*]：大きく丸い目を表す。
Describes big, round eyes.

ノビノビ [*nobi nobi*]：人やものが、せかされたり制限を受けたりすることのない状態。
Suggests that someone or something is not being rushed or subject to constraints.

アクセク [*akuseku*]：休みなく続く仕事や活動。落ち着きのない状態。
A situation of nonstop work, activity or restlessness.

①— **Suku suku** sodatte, mata okiku natta wa ne!（You're growing up so fast! You've gotten bigger again, haven't you?）

②— **Kuri kuri** shita me ga totemo kawaii!（You're so cute with those big, round eyes!）

③— **Nobi nobi** sodate yo to omotte imasu. **Akuseku** shite mo nee..!（We want him to grow up naturally. It's no use for us to push him too much, is it?）

Conditions & Health

健康管理

解説

ホッ [*hot*]：安堵の小さなため息。
 A light sigh of relief.
ガクッ [*gakut*]：失望する様子。
 Describes a feeling of disappointment.
イライラ [*ira ira*]：いらだつ様。
 Describes a feeling of irritation.

① — *Ketsuatsu wa antei shiteimasu ne.* (Your blood pressure is stable.)
 — ***hot***
② — *Demo tabako to arukoru wa dame desu yo.* (But you should refrain from smoking and drinking.)
 gakut
③ — *Jinsei no tanoshimi wa takusan arimasu yo. Tabako to arukoru ga sokokara hette mo wazuka futatsu dake ja arimasen ka...!* (Life has a lot of pleasures. If you stop smoking and drinking, you give up just two pleasures out of many.)
 ira ira

目薬

> **解説**
>
> **ポタ** [*pota*]：水滴が垂れる音。「ポタポタ」は垂れる音が繰り返す様子。
> Describes the sound of a falling drop of water. When repeated, *pota pota* describes a continuous dripping sound.
>
> **シバシバ** [*shiba shiba*]：ゆっくりと何度もまばたきをする様子。
> Describes slow and repeated blinking.
>
> **パチパチ** [*pachi pachi*]：上下のまつ毛が当たる様子。目を連続して開けたり閉じたりすること。
> Describes the action of the upper and lower eyelashes hitting each other, indicating repeated blinks.
>
> **ジッ** [*jit*]：動かない状態。
> Refers to a state of motionless.

① ***pota***
— Domo me ga tsukareru… (My eyes get tired easily.)

② ***shiba shiba***

③ — ***Pachi pachi*** shinai de me o tsumutte shibaraku ***jit*** to shiteru no ga ii no yo. (Rather than blinking a lot, it's better to keep your eyes shut for a little while.)

Conditions & Health

気になる体型

解説

プヨンプヨン [*puyon puyon*]：プヨプヨの強調形。柔らかく弾力性があり、張りがなく垂れた意味合いがある。脂肪が付いた体の表現に使われる。

An emphatic version of *puyo puyo*, which describes a flabby object. The term describes something that is relatively soft and elastic, and sometimes dangling. The term is used to describe a fat body.

ムチムチ [*muchi muchi*]：太っている様子。大柄でぽっちゃりした体形の人に使われるが、必ずしも否定的なニュアンスで使われるわけではない。

Suggests fleshiness. The term may be used to describe a big or plump person, but does not always carry negative connotations.

ガリガリ [*gari gari*]：やせこけた状態を表す。

Describes being skinny.

① *puyon puyon*
② *muchi muchi*
　— Shibo ga tsuite, iya da wa... (Oh no! I've become fat.)
③ — Saikin wa **gari gari** yori hyoka suru hito mo oi rashii yo... (I hear that nowadays people say it's better [to be plump] than skinny.)

湿布

> **ペタッ** [*petat*]：ものを他のものに貼りつける様子。「ペタペタ」はその行動の繰り返しを指す。「ベタッ」「ベタベタ」は，より強力に貼りつく様子。
> Describes adhering something to something else. ***Peta peta*** suggests repeating such an action. ***Betat*** and ***beta beta*** indicate something that adheres more strongly.
>
> **ジワジワ** [*jiwa jiwa*]：露骨に分かるほどではなく，少しずつ進行する様子。
> Suggests something is progressing, not overtly, but little by little.
>
> **ホカホカ** [*hoka hoka*]：程よく温かい感じ。
> Suggests something is moderately warm.
>
> **ヌクヌク** [*nuku nuku*]：体が快適に暖まる様子。
> Indicates the body becoming comfortably warm.

① ***petat***
— *Katakori ni wa kore o haru no ga ichiban!* (These [compresses] are the best way to soothe stiff shoulders.)

② — ***Jiwa jiwa*** *to kiite kuru wa.* (They seem to be gradually working.)

③ ***hoka hoka***
— ***Nuku nuku*** *shite kita.* (They're warming me up.)

Conditions & Health

虫歯

解説

シクシク [*shiku shiku*]：歯や歯肉，胃腸など，内部で鈍痛が続く状態。
Describes dull, repetitive pain felt internally, such as in the teeth, gums, stomach or intestines.

グラグラ [*gura gura*]：本来は固くしっかりしているはずのものが揺れ動いている状態。
Describes something that is supposed to be firm but is now moving.

ポロッ [*porot*]：水滴やボタンなど，小さめのものが下に落ちたり，はずれてしまう状態。
Describes a relatively small thing—such as a drop of water or a button—that suddenly falls down or drops off.

① *shiku shiku*
— Mushiba ga **shiku shiku** suru... (This cavity hurts.)
② — **Gura gura** shiteru! (My tooth's become loose.)
③ — **Porot** to nukenai kana... (I hope the bad tooth will fall out.)

Chapter 6

Fashion & Appearance
ファッション・身だしなみ

Fashion & Appearance

年をとると

① **fusa fusa**
— Au no wa san nen buri da ne... Genki so ja naika.（I haven't seen you for three years. You look well.）
— Demo kuro shiteru yo. Kami mo **suke suke** sa...（But I've been having a hard time. My hair has thinned considerably.）
② — Kaoiro mo yoku, **tsuya tsuya** da ne...（Your complexion is good and glowing...）
— **Shiwa shiwa** ni naru no wa mada hayai sa.（I'm too young to become wrinkled.）
③ **ha ha ha／kapo**
— Otagai ni kimochi dake wa mannen seinen de itai ne...（We would like to be always young at heart...）
④ — Ha wa **gata** ga kiterunda...!!!（My teeth have already become loose.）

解説

フサフサ [*fusa fusa*]：髪の毛が豊かな状態。
　The condition of having a lot of hair.
スケスケ [*suke suke*]：透き通るように薄い様子を指す表現。
　A colloquial expression meaning something is transparently thin.
ツヤツヤ [*tsuya tsuya*]：はりがあって滑らかな状態。
　The condition of being taut and smooth.
シワシワ [*shiwa shiwa*]：シワがたくさんある状態を指す表現。
　A colloquial expression describing the condition of having a lot of wrinkles.
ハハハ [*ha ha ha*]：笑い声。
　Laughing sound.
カポ [*kapo*]：ものが外れた音。この場面では，笑ったときに入れ歯が飛び出した音。
　The sound of something coming off. In this situation, it is the sound of his false teeth popping out as he laughs.
ガタ [*gata*]：老化に関連した問題が起きている状態。
　The condition of having troubles related to aging.

スキンケア

① ― **Zara zara** datta hada ga **sube sube** shitekita wa...!（My rough skin has become so smooth!）
② ― Kono kurimu no sei kana...!?（I think it's because of this cream.）
③ ― **Tsuru tsuru** shite kimochi ga ii...!（My skin's so smooth―it feels so good!）
④ ― Hyojo made **kira kira** kagayaiteru wa!（It makes you look radiant!）

解説

ザラザラ ［*zara zara*］：手触りの粗い様子を指す。
　Describes a rough texture.
スベスベ ［*sube sube*］：手触りが滑らかな様子。
　Describes a smooth texture.
ツルツル ［*tsuru tsuru*］：滑らかでツヤがある様子。
　Describes a smooth, glossy surface.
キラキラ ［*kira kira*］：輝いている様子。類義語の「チカチカ」はまたたくものを指す。「キラキラ」と「チカチカ」は，星の輝き表すのにも使われ，また，「キラキラ」は宝石のような輝きも指す。「目がチカチカする」は，高速の点滅に代表されるような目への刺激を指す。
　It has the meaning of shiny. ***Chika chika*** is used to describe something that blinks. ***Kira kira*** and ***chika chika*** are used to describe blinking stars, and ***kira kira*** also describes the way jewelry sparkles. ***Me ga chika chika suru*** describes eye irritations characterized by rapid blinking.

Fashion & Appearance

オシャレ

① ― **Chara chara** suru mono o mini tsukete...（She's wearing lots of garish gear.）
② ― Kare mo **gin gin** ni kazatteru...!（His clothes are very flashy, too.）
③ ― Boku wa maiasa **zori zori** to hige o sorunoga seiippai no oshare da...（The only thing I do to improve my appearance is to shave in the morning.）
　― Watashi mo...（Me, too...）

解説

チャラチャラ [*chara chara*]：文字通りには，小さな金属片や固いものが互いにぶつかり合う音や，その動きを表す(類:ジャラジャラ)。また，派手で品がなく，うわついた振るまいや格好を指す。この場面では，いずれの意味も含んでいる。
Describes the sound of small metal pieces or other hard items hitting each other, or the appearance of such things in motion. Its synonym is *jara jara*. *Chara chara* is also used to refer to behavior or appearance that is flashy, vulgar or flippant. In this example, both meanings are implied.

ギンギン [*gin gin*]：輝くような派手な外見を指す。
Refers to a shiny, flashy appearance.

ゾリゾリ [*zori zori*]：カミソリで剃る音を指す。
Describes the sound of shaving.

ファッション・身だしなみ

デートの準備

① *zori zori*
② *sukat*
　— *Sappari shita.*（I feel refreshed.）
③ *waku waku*
④ *uki uki*

解説

ゾリゾリ［*zori zori*］：カミソリで剃る音。無精ひげの手触りも指す。
Describes the sound of shaving. The term also refers to the texture of facial stubble.

スカッ［*sukat*］：爽快な感じを表す。
Expresses a refreshing feeling.

ワクワク［*waku waku*］：期待や興奮の感覚を表す。類義語の「ドキドキ」は，心臓が大きく拍動する音を指す。
Describes a feeling of anticipation or excitement. *Doki doki*, its synonym, illustrates the sound of a heart beating heavily.

ウキウキ［*uki uki*］：「ワクワク」と類義語。心が弾んでいる感じ。しばしばセットで使われる。
Synonym of *waku waku*, the term describes a happy feeling. It is often used together with *uki uki*.

Fashion & Appearance

恋の結果

① — *Fasshyon wa **bacchiri**...!* (I look great!)
② — *Kanojo no hato o **gacchiri** itadaki da...!* (She won't be able to resist me!)
③ ***tohoho／gakkuri／tobo tobo***
  — *Furareta...!* (She turned me down!)

解説

バッチリ [*bacchiri*]：物事が正しく行われた様子(例:「準備はできたか？」「バッチリです」)。
Describes something done just right. For example, *Junbi wa dekita ka?* (Are you ready?) — *Batchiri desu.* (I sure am!)

ガッチリ [*gacchiri*]：強い力でつかんだり、ちゃんと捕らえること。
Refers to grasping something with strength or catching something correctly.

トホホ [*tohoho*]：情けない気持ちを表す。
An expression of a miserable feeling.

ガックリ [*gakkuri*]：落胆した様子。
An expression of disappointment.

トボトボ [*tobo tobo*]：気分が沈んでおり、歩みが遅いこと。
Indicates walking slowly while depressed.

ヒゲと髪

① ― Kono **boo boo** no hige mo kibun tenkan ni sotte **sappari** shiyo ka na.
（Maybe I should shave this bushy beard to make myself feel refreshed.）
② ― Demo atama wa usuku naru bakari da.（But my hair is getting thin.）
③ **soyoo**
― Hige wa sotta kedo kami ha soyoide, kibun ga ochitsuka nai naa.（Even though my beard is gone, my hair blows in the wind and I don't really feel better.）

解説

ボーボー [*boo boo*]：伸び放題のヒゲや雑草に使われる（例：空き地に草がボーボー，スネ毛がボーボー）。
Describe things like unruly beards and weeds. Examples are: *Akichi ni kusa ga boo boo*（There are weeds growing all over the vacant lot）, *Sunege ga boo boo*（He has really hairy legs）.

サッパリ [*sappari*]：シンプルで軽やかであり，余計なものや重苦しさ，派手さなどがまったくない様子。逆は「ゴテゴテ」「コテコテ」。
Indicates a situation in which something is simple, light, and not burdened by anything extra, heavy or loud. The opposites of sappari are gote gote and kote kote. Exaggerated forms are **gote gote** and **kote kote**, respectively.

ソヨー [*soyoo*]：風がやさしく吹く様子。
Describes the sound of wind blowing gently.

Fashion & Appearance

ヘアケア

① パサパサ、キシキシしていた髪が…
② これで洗ったらトロ〜ッとした感じになって、それでいてサラッとしているの…
③ そのボサボサ頭に使ってみたら？ ／ 私は私よ…！

① — **Pasa pasa kishi kishi** shite ita kami ga... （My hair is so dry and coarse...）
② — Kore de arattara **torot** to shita kanji ni natte, sorede ite **sarat** to shite iru no. （If you wash it with this, it'll make it soft. It doesn't make it oily, either.）
③ — Sono **bosa bosa** atama ni tsukatte mita ra? （So why don't you use it on your messy hair?）
 — Watashi wa watashi yo...! （Don't tell me what to do. I'll do what I like.）

解説

パサパサ [*pasa pasa*]：輝きや潤いがない様子。
Describes something that fails to shine or lacks moisture.

キシキシ [*kishi kishi*]：乾燥したものやひっかかりやすいものを動かしているような音（類: ギシギシ）。
The sound of something dry and scratchy being moved about. Its synonym, *gishi gishi*.

トローッ [*torot*]：通常は濃くなめらかな液体を表す表現。ここではそのようになめらかな手触りの髪であることを表している。
Describes a thick and smooth liquid. In this situation, it describes liquid-smooth hair.

サラッ [*sarat*]：べたつきや湿り気がなく、なめらかな様子。
Describes something dry, smooth and not sticky.

ボサボサ [*bosa bosa*]：乱れた髪の様子。
Used to describe unkempt hair.

ファッション・身だしなみ

服のサイズ

① ― **Buku buku** futotte shimatta node kirarenaku natta no. Ageruwa. Anata nara **pittari** yo... (I've got so fat, I can't wear this, so I'll give it to you. It should fit you perfectly.)
② ― **Dabu dabu** suru. Nemaki gawari ni suru wa... (It's too loose. I'll use it as a pajama top.)

解説

ブクブク [*buku buku*]：太った体を表す。
Used to describe a fat body.

ピッタリ [*pittari*]：隙間なく密着している様子や，2人の人が完全に同意していたり，複数のものが完璧に一致している様子(例：2人の意見はピッタリ)。
Tightly. The term also describes a situation in which two people or things are in perfect agreement. For example, *futari no iken wa* **pittari**. (the two people have exactly the same opinion.)

ダブダブ [*dabu dabu*]：服や靴などの大きさがゆるい様子(類：ガバガバ，ブカブカ，ユルユル)。
Used to describe loose-fitting clothes, shoes and other items. Synonyms are *gaba gaba*, *buka buka* and *yuru yuru*.

Fashion & Appearance

ひげそり

解説

ペタペタ [*peta peta*]：液状のものを塗り広げたり，紙切れを貼り付けたりする様子。その音も表す。
Describes a situation in which someone is spreading a liquidlike substance or sticking pieces of paper on a flat surface, as well as sounds made from such actions.

ゾリゾリ [*zori zori*]：顔や頭を剃る音。
The sound of shaving one's face or head.

ヒリヒリ [*hiri hiri*]：皮膚や粘膜の表面が持続して刺激を受けて痛い感覚。辛い味にも使う。
Describes the stinging sensation on the skin or membranous areas. It also can indicate a spicy flavor.

ポンポン [*pon pon*]：ものを軽くたたく音。
The sound of lightly slapping something.

① *peta peta*
② *zori zori*
③ *hiri hiri ／ pon pon*
　— Kono afuta-sheibingu-roshon wa shimite itai naa... (This after-shave lotion stings...)

やせなくちゃ

解説

スルッ [surut]：なんの抵抗も感じずに滑らかに動く様子。
Describes a situation in which something can move smoothly without any resistance.

ピッチピチ（ピチピチ） [picchi picchi (pichi pichi)]：服のサイズが小さすぎて，裂けてしまいそうな様子。
Describes material that seems about to split open because the size is too small.

パンパン [pan pan]：この場面では，女性がお尻をたたく音と，ジーンズが体にぴったりしてきつい状態の両方を指す。
In this situation, the term refers to both the sound of the woman slapping her backside and to the skintight state of her jeans.

ダブダブ [dabu dabu]：服がゆったりしていたりサイズが大きすぎたりする様子（類：ユルユル，ブカブカ，ガバガバ）。
Used to describe loose-fitting or oversized clothes. *Yuru yuru*, *buka buka* and *gaba gaba* are synonyms.

① — *Kono jinzu ga* **surut** *to hakenaku natta...!* (I can't get into these jeans anymore!)

② — **Picchi pichi** *da wa...!* (They're so tight!)
   pan pan

③ — **Dabu dabu** *no o haku yori daietto ga kyumu ka na...!?* (Rather than wearing baggy pants, I guess my first priority is to lose some weight.)

Fashion & Appearance

床屋

解説

チョキチョキ [*choki choki*]：ハサミで切る音やその行為を表す。
Describes the sound or action of scissors cutting.

ジョキジョキ [*joki joki*]：これもハサミで切る音を表すが，さらに誇張した語で，もっと大きな音であることを示唆する。
Also describes scissors cutting, but is more exaggerated, implying a larger sound.

バッサリ [*bassari*]：一気に勢いよく，思い切って切りおとすこと。
Describes cutting off something boldly and in one go.

サッパリ [*sappari*]：汚く乱雑な感じがなく，清潔で爽快な感じの状態。
Indicates a clean and refreshed state free from dirt and complications.

スッキリ [*sukkiri*]：爽快感やさわやかな感じを表す。
Indicates a refreshing feeling or flavor.

スカッ [*sukat*]：爽快感を表す。
Describes a refreshed feeling.

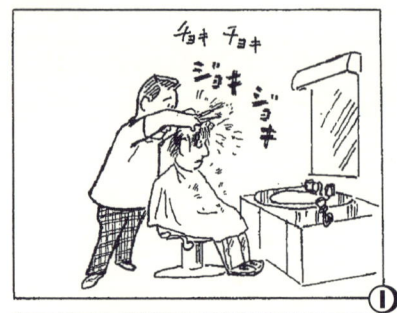

① *choki choki* / *joki joki*
② — Motto **bassari** kitte kudasai...! (Please chop a lot more off!)
③ — Aa, **sappari**, **sukkiri** shita! (Ah, that feels much better!)
sukat

ヘアスタイル

解説

ツンツン [*tsun tsun*]：端が鋭くなっている小さなものや，その鋭い先端が突き出していたり伸びていたりする様子を表す。
Refers to small things with sharp ends, or describes those sharp ends popping up or growing out.

ツルツル [*tsuru tsuru*]：表面が非常に滑らかな様子。
Describes a very smooth surface.

ピカ（ッ） [*pika(t)*]：光のきらめきを表す。「ピカピカ」は，光が持続する様子や，真新しいものを表す。
Refers to a flash of light. *Pika pika* describes continuous glittering, and it also refers to brand-new things.

カーッ [*kaat*]：強い太陽の日差しを表す。
Describes glaring sunlight.

① — **Tsun tsun** shita heasutairu ni shite mitan da...（I have my hair spiky.）
② — Boku wa **tsuru tsuru** ni soreba suzushiku naru to omottan da...（I thought it'd be cooler if I had my head shaved.）
　pika
③ **kaat**
　— Demo, chokusha nikko de atsui, atsui...!（But in this strong sunlight, it's burning hot!）

Fashion & Appearance

体型変化？

解説

ブカブカ [*buka buka*]：覆うべき対象物よりも，ずっと大きい様子。服や靴について使われる。
Indicates that something is much larger than the thing it should cover. Often used for clothes and shoes.

ズル（ッ） [*zuru(t)*]：やや重さのあるものがすべり落ちるさま。
Indicates that something relatively heavy is sliding down.

ギュッギュッ [*gyut gyut*]：ものを詰め込んだり締め付けたりするために繰り返し力をかける様子。
Suggests applying force repeatedly to pack in or tighten up something.

① ***buka buka***
— *Yaseta no kana…?* (Have I lost weight?)

② ***zuru***
— *Beruto no ana o fuyasanakya…* (I'll have to make a new hole in my belt.)

③ ***gyut gyut***
— *Nanka hen da na…* (This isn't going well…)

: ファッション・身だしなみ

エチケット

ピッ [*pit*]：テープや布などを勢いよく剥がしたり裂いたりするときの音。
The sound of tape being peeled off or torn up.

ペタペタ [*peta peta*]：何度も貼ったりはがしたりする音や，くっつきやすく粘着性のあるものが連続して表面に付けられるときの音。
The sound of something repeatedly being stuck to and then removed from, or something adhesive or clingy being repeatedly applied to a surface.

① ― *Chotto matte! Hidoi fuke yo...!*（Wait a second! You're covered in dandruff...!）
② ***pit***
 ― *Nenchaku tepu de totte ageru.*（I'll clean it up with some tape.）
③ ***peta peta***
 ― *Itsumo chui shite inai to dame yo...*（You've always got to be careful.）

Chapter 7

Work & Office
仕事・オフィス

Work & Office

要注意

① — Nanda kono **pera pera** no ripoto wa... (What is this flimsy report?)
② — Nakami mo **pera pera** dane. Kaita yatsu ga **pera pera** no **occhokochoi** nandaro. (The content is weak, too. I bet the writer is shallow and a scatterbrain.)
shiit
③ — Kaita nowa ano kacho da... Soreni kanojo nimo ki o tsukero. Aruku hosokyoku dakara ne. (That section chief wrote it. And watch out for her. Whatever she hears gets passed on immediately.)
suta suta
④ — **Bera bera** to kuchi ga karuin da. (She is a blabbermouth.)

解説

ペラペラ（①）[*pera pera*]：薄い様子。
Thinness.
ペラペラ（②）[*pera pera*]：(内容が) 弱い，浅い，深みに欠ける様子。
Weakness, shallowness, lack of depth.
オッチョコチョイ [*occhokochoi*]：言動が軽々しい人を指す。ただし，「性格的には良い，愉快な人」との含意がある。
Refers to a person who speaks or acts hastily, but implies they are good-natured and amusing.
シーッ [*shiit*]：静かにするよう求める時の表現。
Trying to quiet the atmosphere.
スタスタ [*suta suta*]：足早に歩く様子。
Walking quickly.
ベラベラ [*bera bera*]：しゃべり過ぎる様子。類義語の「ペラペラ」には，外国語を流暢に話す様子に使うなど肯定的なニュアンスがあるが，「ベラベラ」はマイナスイメージの語感。
Talk too much. *Pera pera* is used in a positive sense, such as to describe a person who speaks a foreign language fluently, but *bera bera* has a negative connotation.

不正行為

① *hiso hiso* / *boso boso*
② *koso koso*
　— ?!
③ *shiin*
　— ?!

> **解説**
>
> **ヒソヒソ** [*hiso hiso*]：ささやく様子，小声で話す様子，秘密を話す様子を表す。
> Whispering; speaking in an undertone. Used when people are discussing a secret.
> **ボソボソ** [*boso boso*]：抑えた声で話す様子。「ヒソヒソ」と類義。
> Talking in a subdued tone. A synonym of *hiso hiso*.
> **コソコソ** [*koso koso*]：何かをひそかに行う様子。
> Doing something secretly.
> **シィーン（シーン）** [*shiin*]：静まり返っている様子。しばしば，その場の緊張を示唆する。
> Describes a deafening slience. Often indicates a state of tension.

Work & Office

余分は処分

① **basat**
— *Shobunsuru shorui o shuredda ni kakete kudasai.* (Could you shred these unnecessary documents?)
— *Hai.* (Yes.)

② **zazaza / dosat**
— *Koremo...!* (These, too!)

③ **dokat**
— *Madamada arimasu yo.* (There are still many more.).

④ — *Bunsho o konpyuta ni utsushitara tana ga **sukkiri** shita. Surimu ni naru no wa iikotoda.* (The shelves have become neat, now that we have stored our documents in a computer. It is good to tidy up.)
sukat

解説

バサッ [*basat*]：何か薄くてまとまった量のものが，落ちたり，乱雑に置かれたりする音や様子を表す（類：ドサッ）。
Describes the sound or the state of dropping a bundle of something thin or placing it roughly. (synonym : *dosat*)

ザザザ [*za za za*]：大量の物が何かに当たる音。ここでは，シュレッダーが書類を裁断するときの音。
Describes a large amount of something jammed up against an object. In this case, the sound the shredder makes when cutting up the documents.

ドサッ [*dosat*]：「バサッ」と似ているが，もっと大きく重いものであることを強調した表現。
Similar to *basat* but it emphasizes that the items are bigger and heavier.

ドカッ [*dokat*]：「バサッ」や「ドサッ」よりも重くボリュームがある様子。
More emphatic than *basat* and *dosat* in termes of weight or bulk.

スッキリ [*sukkiri*]：さっぱりとしてすがすがしい状態や空間を表す。
A refreshing condition or space.

スカッ [*sukat*]：爽快な感じを表す。
A refreshing feeling.

仕事・オフィス

危機せまる?!

① **gaan**
　― ...Na, nanda kono kyodaina fusai wa ...!!!（What is this huge debt!）
② ― Kono tsuke wa watashi no kaisya nimo **hita hita** to oshiyosete kurukamo...（This debt might gradually start to affect my company.）
　wana wana
③ ― Ano kigyo no keiei hoshin ga kawatta toki **pin** to kitanda abunaitte ne...（When the company's management policy changed, I got a hunch that the company might be in trouble...）
④ ― Shikashi, toho wa **den** to kamaete yosu o miyo!
　（However, we should stay cool and see what happens!）
　zuru

解説

ガーン [*gaan*]：ショックを受けた状態を指す。
　Describes a state of shock.

ヒタヒタ [*hita hita*]：水が少しずつ身近に迫ってくるように物事が押し寄せる様子。
　Something inches closer, like water moving in.

ワナワナ [*wana wana*]：恐怖や怒りで体が震える様子。
　State of trembling with fear or anger.

ピン [*pin*]：何かがひらめいたり突然分かったときの様子を表す表現。
　Describes an idea coming to mind with a snap, or suddenly understanding something.

デン [*den*]：動じずに安定して穏やかでいること。
　Describes remaining stable, calm.

ズル（ッ） [*zuru(t)*]：飲み物をすする音。
　The sound of sipping a drink.

Work & Office

ピンチはチャンス

① — *Kondo no kaisha mo **bassari** kubi da yo...* (My new company fired me, too.)
② — *Dono kaisha mo boku o **poi** sute nanda...! **Mushakusya** suru kiryoku mo ushinatta yo...* (Every company just dumps me mercilessly...! I have lost the energy to get angry...)
③ — *Boku ga tsukuru no wa toraburu kurai da...! Kubi ni shita kaisya wa dokomo **hot** to shiterusa...* (The only thing I make is trouble. The companies that fired me must have felt relieved to see the back of me...)
   pon
④ — *Sono toraburu ni tsuite hon o dashite minaika? Igai to ureru kamo...!* (Why don't you publish a book about your troubles? It may even sell well...!)
   dote

解説

バッサリ [*bassari*]：一度に勢いよく切断する様子。この場面では，この男性があっけなくクビになったことを指す。「首を切る」は「解雇」の意味。
Describes cutting something with one strong stroke. In this situation, it means he was fired in an offhand manner. *Kubi o kiru*, which literally translates as "behead," means discharge.

ポイ [*poi*]：簡単に無造作に投げ捨てる様子。
Describes throwing something lightly and nonchalantly.

ムシャクシャ [*mushakusya*]：怒りやいらだちの感情であること。
A state of being angry and irritated.

ホッ [*hot*]：安堵した様子。
State of feeling relieved.

ポン [*pon*]：手を軽くたたく音。
The sound of clapping hands.

ドテ [*dote*]：ひっくり返って倒れる様子（ここでは，思いもよらぬアイデアに驚いて）。驚きを強調するために漫画で良く使われる表現。
The state of falling down (in surprise at an unexpected idea in this situation). It is often used to emphasize surprise.

仕事・オフィス

まだまだ現役

① *chaka chaka*
② *sura sura*
 — ...*dekiru!*（He can do it!）
 — *Yatteru...!*（He is doing well...!）
③ — *Madamada wakai mono ni wa makenai yo, geneki no **bari bari** dazo...!!!*（I'm not ready to give in to the younger generation yet. I am still an active worker.）
④ ***bari bari***

解説

チャカチャカ [*chaka chaka*]：素早くタイプ入力する様子やその音。
 Describes typing quickly, or its sound.
スラスラ [*sura sura*]：物事がスムーズに進む様子。
 Describes things going smoothly.
バリバリ [*bari bari*]：精力的に働く様子。
 Describes working hard.

Work & Office

意気込み

① — ...*nige no senryaku wa dame da.* **Gan gan** *semenakya...!* (Running away is not a good strategy. We should be constantly on the attack...!)
② — *Aite wa* **don don** *toshi suru tsumori rashii kara...* (Our rival seems to be planning to invest steadily...)
③ — *Kocchi no pesu de* **gun gun** *hippareba...* (If we take the lead and force them to adjust to our pace...)
⑤ — **Byun byun** *ikeru zo!* (things will really take off!)
　— *Kiiteru dake de tsukareso da...* (I feel tired just listening to you.)

解説

ガンガン [*gan gan*]：活発で勢のある様子。激しい音や，ひどい頭痛を表すときにも使う。
State of being active and having momentum. It is also used to describe a violent noise or an acute headache.

ドンドン [*don don*]：物事が絶えず勢いよく進行する様子。
Describes something progressing steadily with momentum.

グングン [*gun gun*]：力強く勢いのある様子。
State of being powerful with momentum.

ビュンビュン [*byun byun*]：高速で進んだり，回ったりする様子。この場面では，商品が次々に売れて彼らの会社が市場をリードするようになることを表している。
Describes something progressing rapidly or revolving fast. In this situation, it indicates that the goods will sell fast and the company will become an industry leader.

禁煙失敗

① **wana wana**
② **dat**
　— Mo gaman dekinai!（I can't stand it any longer!）
③ **hot／dota dota／moku moku／puka puka／supa supa**
　— mada nakama ga itazo…!（We still have our comrade…!）

解説

ワナワナ [*wana wana*]：大きく震える様子を表す。不安定な精神状態を伴い，落ち着かない気持ちや非常に強い不快感を表す。
Suggests a intense trembling state. ***Wana wana*** is used to imply a shaky mind, evoking a feeling of uneasiness or extreme discomfort.

ダッ [*dat*]：突然駆け出す様子。
Suggests the act of suddenly dashing out.

ホッ [*hot*]：安心した様子。
Describes a feeling of relief.

ドタドタ [*dota dota*]：せわしない様子や，やかましい足音を表す。
The state of being restless or the sound of noisy steps.

モクモク [*moku moku*]：煙や気体がふくれあがる様子。煙突からの煙や大きな雲柱が立ちのぼる様子を表すのによく使われる。
Evokes puffs of smoke or rising gases. Is commonly used to describe chimney smoke or gigantic columns of clouds rising in the sky.

プカプカ [*puka puka*]：ものが軽く浮いている状態。この場面では，タバコの煙が漂う様子を指す。
Suggests that something is floating lightly. In this situation, it describes smoke from a cigarette wafting through the air.

スパスパ [*supa supa*]：タバコを続けざまにふかす動作。
Suggests the act of taking successive puffs on a cigarette.

Work & Office

本音でスッキリ

① *mut* / *zuke zuke*
② *gusat*
③ *kukut* / *suut*

解説

ムッ [*mut*]：腹を立てる様子。
Taking offense.

ズケズケ [*zuke zuke*]：相手の気持ちも考えずに，自分の本音を一方的に話す様子。
A situation in which someone speaks his or her mind on a one-sided basis without considering the other person's feelings.

グサッ [*gusat*]：何かが突き刺さる様子。非常につらい言葉が胸に突き刺さる様子を表すのにも使われる。
The act of being stabbed. It is also used to describe a situation in which a person feels as if he or she has been stabbed through the heart after hearing extremely painful words.

ククッ [*kukut*]：この場面では，悔しさに涙を流す様子を指す。
In this case, the expression describes crying in frustration.

スーッ [*suut*]：気分がすっきりする感じ。この場面では，女性が自分の本音を吐き出したことで気分が良くなり，サッパリした様子を表す。
A refreshing feeling. The woman feels good about herself because she has relieved stress by speaking her mind.

早すぎる？

① **sowa sowa**
— Mosugu haru mo owaru ne... (Spring will end soon.)
② — **Jiwa jiwa** to natsu ga chikazuite iru yo... At to iumani aki ga kuru... (Summer is gradually coming, and then autumn will be here before you know it.)
ira ira
— Zuibun sekkachi da ne... (You sound really impatient about it.)
③ — Gurafikku dezaina to shite wa rainen no karenda no dezain o **bochi bochi** kangae nai to...!
(As a graphic designer, it's time to start considering designs for next year's calendars.)
jiri jiri

解説

ソワソワ [*sowa sowa*]：落ち着かない様子を指す。
Describes a feeling of restlessness.
ジワジワ [*jiwa jiwa*]：物事が少しずつ進行・変化する様子。
Expresses that things are moving slowly or changing slowly.
イライラ [*ira ira*]：物事が思ったようにスムーズに進まないためにいらだちを感じている様子。
Describes being irritated because something is not going as smoothly as expected.
ボチボチ [*bochi bochi*]：物事が少しずつ進捗する様子。
Describes things moving slowly.
ジリジリ [*jiri jiri*]：「イライラ」の類義語。物事が進まない焦燥感を表す。
Synonym of *ira ira*. Describes being frustrated as something is not going smoothly.

Work & Office

出張準備

① — ***Gyuu gyuu*** *zume ni shicha dame yo!* (Don't pack them in so tight!)
　— *Mada hairu yo!* (There's still room for more.)
② — ***Pan pan*** *ja nai no! Baggu o futatsu ni waketa hoga iiwa...* (It's too full. You should divide them into two bags.)
　— *Muri kana...!?* (That may not be possible...)
③ — *Hora, naka no shatsu ga **shiwakucha** ni natteru...!!!* (See, the shirts packed inside are all crumpled...!!!)
　tohoho

解説

ギュウギュウ [*gyuu gyuu*]：物が詰め込まれて隙間がない様子(例：ラッシュアワーの通勤電車はいつもギュウギュウだ)。

Expresses packing something too tight with no space left. *Rasshu awa no tsukin densha wa itsumo **gyuu gyuu** da.* (Commuter trains during rush hour are always packed.)

パンパン [*pan pan*]：満杯ではじけそうな様子(例：食べ過ぎておなかがパンパン)。

Describes something so full that it's about to burst. *Tabesugi te onaka ga **pan pan**!* (I ate too much — I'm stuffed!)

シワクチャ [*shiwakucha*]：シワだらけになっている様子。シワは「皺」のことで、クチャは形がくずれて乱れた状態のものを表す「クチャクチャ」や「グチャグチャ」から来ている。「シワグチャ」とは言わない。シワクチャは、お年寄りの皺だらけの顔を侮蔑的ニュアンスで表す場合にも使う。

Refers to something being crumpled. *Shiwa* means wrinkles. *Kucha* comes from *kucha kucha* and *gucha gucha*, both of which describe the state of being out of shape or in disarray. However, we don't say *shiwagucha*. *Shiwakucha* is sometimes used to refer to the very wrinkled faces of the elderly in a somewhat contemptuous way.

トホホ [*tohoho*]：落ち込んだり、情けなく思っている様子を表す。

Indicates that someone feels depressed or sorry for himself.

不景気

① — *Uwaa! Mata kabuka ga **gakun** to sagatta.* (Oh my God! Stock prices have fallen hard again!)
② — *Kanren gaisha wa **bata bata** tosan suru shi...* (Our affiliated companies are going bankrupt one after another...)
③ — *Uchi no kaisya mo **appu appu** shiterunda...! Taitanikku-go no senkyaku kibun sa. Boku nado funayoi no Dikapurio dayo.* (My company is also on the verge of going down. I feel like a passenger aboard the Titanic. I'm a seasick [Leonardo] DiCaprio [who plays the hero in the movie "Titanic"]).
— *Nite inai...!* (You don't look anything like him.)

解説

ガクン [*gakun*]：急に下がる様子。
Expresses the state of things suddenly going down, or the sound made in such a situation.

バタバタ [*bata bata*]：非常に忙しい様子や，ものが次から次へと倒れる様子を指す。
Describes hectic action or things falling down suddenly one after another.

アップアップ [*appu appu*]：おぼれそうになっている様子や，その比喩で困難で苦しい状況を表す。
Refers to a situation in which someone is about to be drowned. It is also used as a metaphor for a difficult situation.

Work & Office

栄養ドリンク

解説

グビッ [*gubit*]：飲み物を一度に勢いよく飲む様子やその音。
Describes the act or sound of swallowing liquid in one breath.

スカッ [*sukat*]：気分転換してリフレッシュした様子(類: スッキリ)。
Refers to feeling refreshed. ***Sukkiri*** is a synonym.

モリモリ [*mori mori*]：元気で力強いさま。
Describes an uplifting force.

① — *Natsubate da. Dorinkuzai o nonde genki o tsuke yo.* (This summer heat is really getting me down. An energy drink will perk me up.)

② ***gubit***

③ ***sukat* / *mori mori***
— *Terebi CM no anji ni kakariyasui seikaku nanda ne…!* (You're too easily influenced by TV commercials.)

疲れたら

> **解説**
>
> **ショボショボ** [*shobo shobo*]：目が疲れて開けられず，まばたきする様子。
> Describes not being able to open one's eyes due to fatigue and blinking one's eyes.
>
> **コリコリ** [*kori kori*]：肩がこって固くなっているさま。
> It is used to describe stiff shoulders.
>
> **ゴクッ** [*gokut*]：液体を飲み込む音。この場面では唾液。
> The sound of swallowing liquid — in this case, saliva.

① — *Me ga **shobo shobo** suru...* (My eyes are bleary.)

② ***kori kori***
— *Kata mo koru shi...* (My shoulders are getting stiff.)

③ — *Hatarakisugi ni chigai nai! Nonde iru toki wa genki dakara...!!!* (Having a drink would feel great after working so hard!)
gokut

Work & Office

一段落

① **kata kata**
② — ...Kore de kyo no sagyo wa ichidanraku... (That's all for today...)
　chon
③ **hot / patan**

解説

カタカタ [*kata kata*]：タイピング入力する音。
The sound of typing.

チョン [*chon*]：物事の区切りがついた様子。この語はそもそも，芝居の幕を下ろす際に拍子木が鳴る音を表すのに使われていた。この漫画のコマでは，一番最後のタイピング音と，その日の仕事が終了したことの両方を表している。
It indicates the end of an segment. The term was initially used to describe the sound made by wooden clappers when the curtain fell at the end of a play. In the case of this comic strip, the term both refers to the sound of hitting the final key and the end of the day's work.

ホッ [*hot*]：緊張からの解放や安堵感を表す。
Indicates freeing from tension or a feeling of relief.

パタン [*patan*]：比較的うすくて軽いものが倒れたり閉まったりするときの音。
The sound of something relatively thin and light falling or closing.

仕事・オフィス

パソコン習得

解説

スラスラ [*sura sura*]：行動や物事を円滑に行う様子。「サラサラ」は円滑な流れを指し，「ペラペラ」は流暢に話す様子。
Describes actions or other events that progress smoothly. **Sara sara** is used for something that has a smooth flow to it, while **pera pera** means speaking fluently.

バッチリ [*bacchiri*]：物事が上手く行われた様子。
Describes something done well.

チャカチャカ [*chaka chaka*]：ここでは，キーボードをたたく音と同時に，少年の集中力と素速い手さばきを表し，二つの意味を持たせている。「カチャカチャ」は主に音を表すが，「チャカチャカ」のほうがより速さを表す。
In this case it describes both the sound of typing on the keyboard as well as the state of the boy's concentration and quick hand coordination, giving it a double meaning. **kacha kacha** can be used to describe the sounds only, although **chaka chaka** gives a greater impression of speed.

① — *Pasokon ni nareta?* (Have you gotten used to your computer?)
— *Mada **sura sura** to wa ikanai ne.* (Things still don't go as smoothly as I'd like.)

② — *Kono baai wa do suruno kana?* (What should I do in this case?)
— *Soko o kurikku suru n da yo.* (You just click that.)

③ — *Kore de **bacchiri** da yo, ojiichan.* (Now it's fine, grandpa.)
chaka chaka
— !?

最近の調子は

トントン [*ton ton*]：二つのものが大体同じ状態を表し，主として収支を表現する場合に使われる。物事が概ね順調に進んでいる場合にも使われる。

Refers to two things that are almost the same. It is usually used to describe a balance of payments. The term also can describe a situation in which something is progressing smoothly.

ジワジワ [*jiwa jiwa*]：物事がゆっくり，しかし確実に進行，または浸透する様子。「ジワッ（と）」「ジワリ」は少量の液体が浸透する様子や，物事が少しだけ進行する様子を表す。

Describes a situation in which something is progressing or permeating steadily but at a slow pace. *Jiwat*(*to*), or *jiwari*, refers to a state in which just a small amount of liquid is permeating into something, or something makes little progress.

① — *Shigoto wa umaku itteru kane?* (Is your business doing OK?)
② — *Ma, shushi wa **ton ton** da.* (Well, it's breaking even.)
③ — *Demo, jidai ya shakai no henkaku o **jiwa jiwa** kanjiru yo...* (But I'm gradually realizing that the times and society are changing.)

Chapter 8

Weather & Climate
天気・気候

Weather & Climate

雨の日には

① *shito shito* / *pasha pasha*
② — *Zubon wa **gusho gusho** da!* (My trousers are dripping wet!)
   pota pota
③ — *Tsukin niwa kawazuri sutairu ga ichiban!* (The best way to commute in the rain is to wear river fishing gear!)
   kyoton
   — ?!

解説

シトシト [*shito shito*]：小雨が静かに降るさま。
　Indicates light rain falling quietly.

パシャパシャ [*pasha pasha*]：水面に物があたって，水が飛び散る様子やその音。
　バシャバシャより軽い感じを表す。
　The sound or condition of something hitting the water surface.

グショグショ [*gusho gusho*]：非常に濡れているさま。
　A condition of extreme wetness.

ポタポタ [*pota pota*]：水滴がたくさん落ちる様子，またはその音。
　The sound or condition of many drops of water falling.

キョトン [*kyoton*]：驚きであっけに取られた様子(類: ポカン)。
　A state of blank amazement. A synonym for *pokan*.

ately # 暑い時には

① — *Achii! Hayaku aki ni naranai kana.* (It's really hot! I wish autumn would come soon.)
② — *Dara dara aruki wa yokei ni atsusa o kanjiru yo.* (Walking slowly makes you feel even hotter.)
  tara tara / **bota bota**
③ — *Shakit to shite kaze o kiruyoni sassa to arukeba...* (It's better to walk briskly as if you were cutting through the wind.)
  suta suta
④ — *...demo shingo de tomatta totan ni...!!!* (...however, as soon as you stop at a traffic light...)
  dobaa

解説

ダラダラ [*dara dara*]：怠けていること。
  Condition of being lazy.
タラタラ [*tara tara*]：汗が立て続けに流れ落ちるさま。
  Describes sweat running down continuously.
ボタボタ [*bota bota*]：大きな滴がしたたり落ちる様子やその音。類義のポタポタは、比較的滴が小さく軽い感じを表す。
  Describes big drops of liquid falling down. A synonym for **pota pota**, which refers to smaller, ligter drops of liquid falling down.
シャキッ [*shakit*]：引き締まって緊張感のある様子。
  Describes being brisk and tense.
サッサ [*sassa*]：素早く動いたり何かをこなしたりする様子(類: テキパキ)。
  Describes moving or doing something quickly. Synonymous with **tekipaki**.
スタスタ [*suta suta*]：足早に歩く様子を表す。
  Describes the state of walking fast.
ドバアア（ドバーッ） [*dobaa (t)*]：液体が急に一気に流れ出すこと。またはそのような時の音。
  Describes a sudden, heavy flow of liquid, or the sound it makes.

Weather & Climate

好きな季節

① — *Aki no kehai ne, atsusa ni yowai watashi wa **hot** to suru wa.*（Autumn is just around the corner. It's a relief for me, as I don't stand up to the heat very well.）
② — *Watashi wa natsu ga suki! Samukute **gata gata** furueru mainichi nante iya yo.*（I like summer. I hate cold, shivery days.）
③ — *Ase de **beta beta** shita hada mo **sarat** to shite kimochi ga iiwa.*（My skin feels nice and dry after being sticky with sweat.）
④ — *Watashi wa hada ga **kasa kasa** ni naru noga iya nanoyo.*（I don't like my skin getting dry.）
pui／mut

解説

ホッ [*hot*]：安堵した状態。
Condition of feeling relieved.

ガタガタ [*gata gata*]：体が激しく震えるさま（類：ブルブル）。
Describes a body shaking violently. A synonym for *buru buru*.

ベタベタ [*beta beta*]：粘着性がある様子。
Describes something sticky.

サラッ [*sarat*]：湿気がなく乾いた状態。
Dry, free from moisture.

カサカサ [*kasa kasa*]：肌などが乾いているさま。
Describes something dry such as skin.

プイ [*pui*]：（不愉快に感じて）顔をそむけるさま。
Describes turning one's face away（because of an unpleasant feeling）.

ムッ [*mut*]：不愉快に感じるさま。「ムカッ」は更にひどく不愉快な気持ちを表す。
Describes an unpleasant feeling. *Mukat* is used to describe an even more unpleasant feeling.

天気・気候

雪かき

① — *Yuki ga* **chira hora** *futte kita.* (It has begun to snow a little.)
   — *Konya wa tsumori sone.* (It probably will settle tonight.)
② — *Ame to chigatte...ato no yukikaki ga taihendayo ne...* (It's different from rain...shoveling up the snow afterward is hard work.)
   saku saku ／ zakut
③ **basat ／ dosat**
   — *Kore da mono ne...!!!* (See what I mean!!!)

解説

チラホラ [*chira hora*]：小さい物が不規則に落ちている様子。「ヒラヒラ」は薄く軽い物に対して使われ，雪が降る様子を表すのには使われない。
Describes small things falling down irregularly. The synonym *hira hira* is used when the things referred to are thin and light. *Hira hira* is not used to describe snow falling.

サクサク [*saku saku*]：比較的軽くて細かい粒状のものが割れたり壊れたりするときの音や様子。ここでは雪かきをしている時の音を表す。「サクッ」の連続・反復表現。
The sound or condition of something light or finely granulated crumbling. In this case, it describes the sound made when shoveling snow.

ザクッ [*zakut*]：粗くてかたい粒状のものが崩れたりするときの音。
The sound of something hard or granulated crumbling.

バサッ [*basat*]：大量のものが落ちて崩れるさま。またはその時の音。
Describes something large falling and collapsing, or the sound of these movements.

ドサッ [*dosat*]：「バサッ」と似ているが，「ドサッ」は物の重さを強調する。
Similar to *basat*, but emphasizes the weight of the object.

Weather & Climate

雪の上

① **zakut zakut**
— *Yuki no ue o arukuto ironna oto ga suru ne...* (When we walk on snow, it creates a lot of different sounds.)
② **kyut kyut**
③ — *At!* (*Aaargh!*)
— *?!*
zubot

解説

ザクッ [*zakut*]：比較的粗く固い粒状のものが壊れたり崩れたりする時の音や様子。
The sound or condition of something relatively rough or a hard granular thing breaking or crumbling.

キュッキュッ [*kyut kyut*]：擦れてきしむような音。
Creaking sound.

ズボッ [*zubot*]：穴などの中にはまり込んだ時の状態やその音。
The sound or state of something getting stuck in a hole.

季節のうつろい

①
- 珍しくポカポカ陽気だね…
- 明日はまた冷えそう。冬将軍はまだ撤退しそうにないわ…

②
- トットと去って早く春と交替してほしいよ…
- 春だってモタモタしてるわけじゃないわ

③
- 毎年そうだけど、春だと思ってるうちにドドッと夏が来て、アッという間に秋になり、冬が…
- きょうと同じか…?!

① ― Mezurashiku **poka poka** yoki da ne... （It's unusually warm today.）
　― Ashita wa mata hieso. Fuyushogun wa mada tettai shiso ni nai wa... （It seems tomorrow will be cold again. General Winter doesn't seem to be about to retreat yet.）

② ― **Totto** to satte hayaku haru to kotai shite hoshi yo. （I wish General Winter would leave quickly so spring could take over.）
　― Haru datte **mota mota** shiteru wake ja nai wa. （I don't think spring is coming slowly on purpose.）

③ ― Mainen so dakedo, haru dato omotteruuchini **dodot** to natsu ga kite, at to iumani aki ni nari, fuyu ga... （It is the same every year, but while we are enjoying spring, summer rushes in and autumn comes in no time, and then winter...）
　― Kyo to onaji ka...?! （Just like today?!）

解説

ポカポカ [*poka poka*]：心地よく暖かい状態。
　State of being comfortably warm.

トット [*totto*]：素早く。去る・消えるなどを相手に求める場合に使う。
　Quicky. The term is used to demand someone to leave or disappear immediately.

モタモタ [*mota mota*]：物事が順調に進まないこと（類：グズグズ）。
　Describes something that doesn't go smoothly. A synonym for *guzu guzu*.

ドドッ [*dodot*]：物事が一気に押し寄せること。
　Describes something rushing in all at once or all together.

Weather & Climate

もうすぐ春が

① — Nissho jikan ga nagaku natte kita. Haru ga **jiwa jiwa** chikazuiteiru... (The days are getting longer. Spring is approaching little by little.)
② — Sono ashioto mo **bochi bochi** kikoeso... (I can almost hear the sound of its steps.)
③ — **Soro soro**...to iu kehai! (I can almost sense spring in the air.)

解説

ジワジワ [*jiwa jiwa*]：物事が少しずつ進んだり，変化したりしている状態。
　The state of something moving or changing gradually.

ボチボチ [*bochi bochi*]：物事が少しずつ起ったり行われる様子。
　An event developing gradually.

ソロソロ [*soro soro*]：間もなく予想される状態になる様子。
　Describes a situation in which something evolves to what one expects.

厳しい暑さ

① **kaat**
② ― *Kyo mo **kan kan** deri da ne...* （It's scorching today again...）
　　― *Shitsudo mo takai yo...* （Humidity is high, too...）
③ ― ***Jito jito**, **jime jime**...* （It's very humid and muggy...）
　　― ***Mun mun** suru ne.* （It's stuffy.）
④ ― *...mada shigotochu dakara nomu wake ni mo ikanai...* （We're still on duty so we can't drink now...）
　　gokut

解説

カーッ [*kaat*]：強烈な日差しが降り注ぐさま。
Describes the sun beating down fiercely.

カンカン [*kan kan*]：焼けつくような太陽の強い光を表す(類: ギラギラ, ジリジリ)。「ギラギラ」は太陽が容赦なく照りつけるさまを表し，「ジリジリ」はやけどしそうなほど強烈な日差しを表す。
Describes the scorching of the sun, and is synonymous with **gira gira** and *jiri jiri*. **Gira gira** suggests that the sun is glaring down relentlessly and *jiri jiri* describes the state of almost being burned by merciless sunshine.

ジトジト [*jito jito*]：空気中の湿気が多いためにくっつくような感じがすること。
Describes the feeling of stickiness due to a lot of moisture in the air.

ジメジメ [*jime jime*]：非常に湿気があるさま。
State of being extremely watery or damp.

ムンムン [*mun mun*]：熱やにおいが充満している様子。
Sense of being enveloped by heat or a smell.

ゴクッ [*gokut*]：液体を飲み込む音。ここではつばを飲み込んでいる。
The sound of swallowing liquid. In this case, he swallows his own saliva.

Weather & Climate

秋晴れ

> 秋空のブルーは何と美しいんだろう…！

sukaan
― *Akizora no buru wa nan to utsukushi n daro...!* (The blue of the autumn sky is so beautiful!)

解説

スカーン [*sukaan*]：抜けるような空の広さとその鮮明な感じを強調している表現。
Emphasizes the vastness of the sky and its refreshingness.

大雨

① *zaaa*
② *hita hita*
　—Taihen! Doa no shita kara shinsui shite kita!!（Oh no! There's water seeping under the door!!）
③ *saaa*
　—Benechia kanko da to omoeba...（Just think of it as sightseeing in Venice...）
　—Nani o nonki na koto o itteru no yo?!（Why are you so calm about it!?）

解説

ザアアア（ザーッ）［*zaaa(zaat)*］：豪雨やその時の音を表す。
Expresses a downpour or the sound of one.

ヒタヒタ［*hita hita*］：水などが少しずつ迫ってくる様子を表す。また，何かを浸す時のかぶる程度の水を表すこともある（例：乾燥した食材をヒタヒタの水で戻す）。
Describes something approaching, particularly water. Can also describe a small amount of water that barely covers something. For example, *Kansoshita shokuzai o **hita hita** no mizu de modosu*（Reconstitute dried foods in a small amount of water that barely covers the ingredients）.

サアアア（サーッ）［*saaa(saat)*］：ここでは「ザアアア」より雨の量が少なく，勢いも弱いことを示す。
In this situation, *saaa* denotes a smaller quantity and force of rain than *zaaa*.

Weather & Climate

通り雨

解説

ポツポツ [*potsu potsu*]：小さな形の物が散らばっていることを表すことが多い。ここでは，小さな雨粒を指す。
Often refers to the arrangement of small shapes. In this situation, it describes small drops of rain.

ザアアー（ザーッ） [*zaaa(zaat)*]：小さな物が大量に落ちるさま。または，そのような状況での音。ここでは豪雨を表す。
Indicates a large amount of small objects that are falling, or the sound made in such a situation. Here, it describes the sound of a downpour.

ボタボタ [*bota bota*]：類義語「ポタポタ」と共に，水滴が落ちる時の音を表す。「ボタボタ」の方が水滴が大きいことを示す。
Along with its synonym, *pota pota*, *bota bota* can be used to describe the plunking sound of waterdrops falling. *Bota bota* suggests bigger waterdrops.

ピタッ [*pitat*]：継続していた動きや行動が突然，完全に止まる様子。
Describes a continuous movement or action that comes to a sudden and complete stop.

① *potsu potsu*
② *zaaa* ／ *bota bota*
③ *pitat*
— *Toriame da...* (It was a passing shower.)

夏の日差し

> **解説**
>
> **カラカラ** [kara kara]：非常に乾いた状態。
> Describes very dry conditions.
>
> **カンカン** [kan kan]：夏の太陽の強い光を表す。
> Refers to the strong light given off by the summer sun.
>
> **チリチリ** [chiri chiri]：暑い天気にさらされたことによる皮ふの痛みを表す。この文脈では、「ジリジリ」や「ヒリヒリ」が同様の意味で使える。
> Describes itchy skin resulting from exposure to hot weather. *Jiri jiri* and *hiri hiri* are synonyms in this context.

① — **Kara kara** tenki da ne... (It's so dry out today.)
② — **Kan kan** deri de... (The sun's rays are so strong...)
③ — Hada ga **chiri chiri** suru wa... (My skin is itchy...)

秋雨

① *shobo shobo*
② *shito shito* / *poto poto* / *picha picha*
③ — Hito ame goto ni aki ga fukamatte ikun da na... (Every time it rains, it seems that autumn has really set in.)
shinmiri

解説

ショボショボ [*shobo shobo*]：弱い雨が寂しげに降る様子。
It describes pensive drizzling rain.

シトシト [*shito shito*]：「ショボショボ」の類義語で弱い雨が降りつづいている様子。
A synonym of *shobo shobo*, the term describes continuous, quiet rain.

ポトポト [*poto poto*]：この場面での雨粒のように、小さな滴が連続して落ちる様子を表す。また、そのような時の音(類: ポタポタ)。
Describes a situation in which small drops keep falling one after another — like drops of rain in this situation. The term also is used to refer to similar sounds. *Pota pota* is a synonym.

ピチャピチャ [*picha picha*]：水滴が跳ね上がる時の音。より大きな音を表す「ビチャビチャ」は濡れた状態を表すのにも使われる。
The sounds made when drops of water splash up from the ground. *Bicha bicha*, which indicates a louder sound, is used to describe the condition of being wet.

シンミリ [*shinmiri*]：静かな、落ち着いた深い気持ちを表す(類: シミジミ)。
Describes a calm settled or deep feeling. *Shimijimi* is its synonym.

天気・気候

春一番

すごい突風だね…！
グオオオォォ

春が **アタフタ** と
かけ抜けているんだよ…
ヒュルルル

夏はすぐ来るさ。秋も冬も
すぐに来て，**アッ** と言う間に
今年も終るよ…
セカセカ

① **Guoooo**
— Sugoi toppu da ne...! (It's a gusty wind, isn't it?)
② **hyurururu**
— Haru ga ata futa to kakenukete irun da yo... (It looks like spring is in a hurry to rush away.)
③ — Natsu wa sugu kuru sa. Aki mo fuyu mo sugu ni kite, **at** to iu ma ni kotoshi mo owaru yo... (Summer is coming soon, so are autumn and winter. This year will be over quite soon.)
seka seka

解説

グオオオオ（グオーッ） [guoooo (guoot)]：強風が作り出す音。
The sound produced by a strong wind.

アタフタ [ata futa]：気持ちが落ち着かず，急いで行動する様子を表す(類: セカセカ)。
Describes a situation in which someone feels ill at ease and acts in a hurry. *Seka seka* is a synonym.

ヒュルルル [hyurururu]：冷たい風が吹くさまを描写する表現として一般的な「ヒュー」の一種で，風の早さなどが変化している様子を表す。
A variation of *hyuu*—a common expression to describe how a cold window blows—*hyurururu* describes the sound produced by a wind whose speed is changing.

アッ [at]：「アッと言う間に」で物事が一瞬で起きることを表す。「アッ」は驚きを表す間投詞として使われる。
At to iu ma ni means something happening in a moment. *At* is used as an interjection for surprise.

セカセカ [seka seka]：急いでいる印象を与える行動や態度を表す。類義語の「スタスタ」は早く歩く様子を表す。
Describes a behavior and attitude that gives the impression of being in a hurry. Its synonym, **suta suta**, refers to walking faster.

Weather & Climate

足下注意

① — *Kosame kara mizore ni natta...!* (This light rain has turned into sleet.)
   bisha bisha／pisha pisha
② **shari shari**
   — *Romen ga toketsu shiso de iya da ne.* (The roads look like they'll freeze over. It's going to be horrible.)
③ **zurut**
   — *Otto...! Kore dakara nee...* (Oops! This is just what I mean.)

解説

ビシャビシャ [*bisha bisha*]：水たまりなどの水面で水滴が跳びはねるさま。またはそのような場面での音(類バシャバシャ)。

Describes drops of water splashing on the surface of a puddle, or similar sounds heard in similar situations. Synonym for *basha basha*

ピシャピシャ [*pisha pisha*]：「ビシャビシャ」と似ているが，水滴がより小さく，音が軽い意味合いがある(類：パシャパシャ，パチャパチャ，ピチャピチャ)。

A close synonym of *bisha bisha*, but it suggests lighter drops and higher sounds than *bisha bisha*. Synonym for *pasha pasha*, *pacha pacha*, *picha picha*.

シャリシャリ [*shari shari*]：固く小さな粒が接触し摩擦する時の音やその状態。ここでは，みぞれを踏みつぶしている音。

The sound or state of hard, fine particles coming into contact with one other. In this case, the term describes the sound of sleet being crushed underfoot.

ズルッ [*zurut*]：重い物を引きずるさま，またはその時の音。人が滑る時の表現としてよく使われる。

Refers to the dragging of a heavy object or its sound. The term is often used to describe a slip of the foot.

雨やどり

ドンヨリ [*donyori*]：暗く重苦しいこと。曇り空や，生気のない目や表情を表すのに使われる。
Something dark and somber. The term can be used to describe an overcast sky, and also glassy eyes or faces.

ポツポツ [*potsu potsu*]：小さな物が点在していること。小さな雨の滴が降り始める時に使われる。
Describes small things scattered. The term can be used when small drops of rain begin to fall.

パラパラ [*para para*]：小さく軽い物が散らばる様子。または，散らばる時の音。
Description of small and light things that are scattered, or the sounds made in such a situation.

ザーッ [*zaat*]：雨や風，水が激しく吹きつけるときの音を表す。大量の粒状の物が一度に動く時にも使われる。
Describes the sound of rain, wind or water beating hard. The term is also used when a large amount of granular objects move at one time.

① *donyori*
  —!?
② *potsu potsu ／ para para*
③ *zaat*

Chapter 9

Seasons & Nature
季節・自然

Seasons & Nature

春の訪れ

ニョキニョキ [*nyoki nyoki*]：長く細い物が急に大きくなること。またはそのような物がたくさん現れること。
Describes long, thin objects growing quickly or many such objects appearing.

フックラ [*fukkura*]：丸まるとして柔らかい質感の物を表す。
Indicates something plump with a soft texture.

ホンノリ [*honnori*]：かすかな色やにおい，味わいを表す。好意的な意味。
Favorably expresses faint colors, smells and tastes.

① — Shinme ga **nyoki nyoki** dete kita! (Look at all the new shoots sprouting!)
② — Kono tsubomi mo **fukkura** shite mo sugu kaika suru ne. (These buds are getting quite big. They'll be blooming soon.)
③ — Kono hana wa **honnori** amai kaori! Hora ne …! (These flowers have a gentle and sweet fragrance. Can you smell them?)

季節・自然

釣り日和

① *sukaan*
② *kira kira*
③ ― Hora ... uki ga **piku piku** shiteru wa ... kakatteirunokana ... （Look! The float is bobbing. I wonder if a fish is hooked.）
gokukt

解説

スカーン [*sukaan*]：すっきりとして澄んだ，広い空間を表す。5月や秋に多く見られる快晴の青い空を描写するのによく使われる。
Describes a refreshing, clear wide space. It is often used to describe the cloudless blue sky which is often seen in May and autumn in Japan.

キラキラ [*kira kira*]：川面などで見られるように，反射したりちらつく光を表す。
Describes reflecting and flickering light, such as light reflecting on the surface of a river.

ピクピク [*piku piku*]：小刻みに動く様子。
Describes something moving bit by bit.

ゴクッ [*gokut*]：液体を飲み込む時の音。
Sound of gulping fluid.

Seasons & Nature

俳句

① **pyon**
② **chapot**
③ **sara sara**
  — *Furuike ya kawazu tobikomu mizu no oto* (A frog jumps into an old pond. The sound of water.)
④ **shiin**

解説

ピョン [*pyon*]：小さな物が飛び跳ねる動きを表す。
Describes the action of a small thing leaping nimbly.

チャポツ [*chapot*]：水面に何か小さなものが投げこまれた時の音（類：ポチャッ, ポチャン, チャポン）。
Sound heard when something small is thrown into a pool of water. There are a number of expressions describing this sound, according to the size or amount of things that fall in. Synonymous with **potchat**, **potchan** and **chapon**.

サラサラ [*sara sara*]：よどみなく流れる物や、表面が乾いて快適な様子を表す。ここでは躊躇せず、筆を止めずに俳句をしたためたことを意味する。
Describes something that flows smoothly or something that is light and dry. In this situation, it means that the man writes the poem without hesitation or stopping. The poem is a famous haiku written by Matsuo Basho (1644-1694).

シーン [*shiin*]：水を打ったような静けさを表す。
Describes complete silence.

猛暑

クーラーをひかえて電気代を節約だ…。窓を開けて風を入れよう…

①

うわ〜ッ

②

照り返しの熱風が強烈だア〜ッ！！！

③

解説

ムーッ [*muut*]：空気が不快な暑さや湿度, においで充満していて息がしにくいほどであるさま。
Suggests that the air is filled with uncomfortable heat, humidity or bad odors, making it difficult for people to breathe.

ドドド／ドバァ [*do do do/dobaa*]：大量の水（ここでは汗）が流れ出す様子。
Expresses a large volume of water gushing out.

① — *Kura o hikaete denkidai o setsuyaku da ... Mado o akete kaze o ire yo ...* (Let's save on the electricity by not using the air conditioner. I'll open the window to let a breeze in.)
② **muut**
— *Uwaaa ...* (Oh, my goodness.)
③ — *Terikaeshi no neppu ga kyoretsu da ...!!* (The hot air is intense due to the reflected heat of the sun.)
　do do do ／ dobaa

Seasons & Nature

さわやか

解説

ムッ [*mut*]：暑くて湿った空気を表す。怒りや不機嫌さを表すこともある。
Indicates hot and humid air. The term also describes anger or displeasure.

カラッ [*karat*]：余分な水分や油分がなく乾いた状態を表す。
Describes something that is dry without excessive moisture and oil.

スカッ [*sukat*]：ふさがれた物が解放されたような，すっきりした気分を表す。
Suggests a refreshing feeling as if something that has been blocked up has been removed.

サラサラ [*sara sara*]：べたつきがなく滑らかな様子。
Indicates a smooth sensation without any hindrance.

① — *Kino wa **mut** to shita atsusa datta no ni, kyo wa **karat** to shiteru wa ne.* (It was humid and hot yesterday, but it's dry today.)
 sukat
② — *Zekko no sentakubiyori ne.* (It's a perfect day for laundry.)
③ — *Hada mo **sara sara** shiteru!* (My skin has become smooth.)

台風

① hyuuuu ／ zawa zawa
② para para para ／ picha picha
③ do do do do ／ zapat

解説

ヒュウウウ [*hyuuuu*]：風が非常に強く吹く音。
The sound of a strong wind blowing.
ザワザワ [*zawa zawa*]：木の葉が風で揺れて立てる音。
The sound of swaying leaves blown by the wind.
パラパラ [*para para*]：大粒の雨が降り出した時の音。
The sound of big drops of rain starting to fall.
ピチャピチャ [*picha picha*]：水滴が跳びはねる音。
The sound of water drops splattering.
ドドドド [*do do do do*]：ここでは大量の水が押し寄せる音。
The sound of a large amount of water flowing forth.
ザパッ [*zapat*]：大量の水が何かにぶつかった音。
The sound of a large amount of water hitting something.

Seasons & Nature

雲

解説

ポッカリ [*pokkari*]：比較的大きく軽いものが空に浮かんでいる様子を表す。この場面での雲や満月がその例。穴が空いている様子にも使われ、比ゆ的な使い方で空虚感や不足感も意味する（例：時間がポッカリ空いた）。

Describes a relatively large, light object floating in the sky, referring, for example, to a cloud like in this scene, or to a full moon. The term also describes a large gaping hole. In a metaphoric usage, *pokkai* also refers to emptiness or something lacking. *jikan ga pokkari aita* means "I found myself with some spare time."

フワフワ [*fuwa fuwa*]：軽くて柔らかい様子。

Refers to something fluffy.

① ***pokkari***
— Ano kumo wa yufo mitaina katachi da ne ... （That cloud looks like a UFO, doesn't it?)

② — ***Fuwa fuwa*** no ofuton no yo ni natte iku ... (Its shape is becoming like a fluffy futon.)

季節・自然

冬の小川

① — Hora, mizu ga **kon kon** to waiteiru! (Look! The water flows constantly.)
choro choro
② — Te o hitashite itara **kiin** to tsumetaku natte kita ... (I soaked my hand in cold water for a while and now it is numb.)
— Demo, wakimizu wa fuyu demo koranai no yo. (However, spring water does not freeze even in winter.)
③ **sara sara**
— **Kakin kokin** ni kotta suimen no shita o zutto nagaretsuzukeruno. (The water continues to flow beneath the rigidly frozen surface.)

解説

コンコン [*kon kon*]：絶えず水がわき出ている様子を表す一般的な表現。
Common phrase to describe constantly flowing water.

チョロチョロ [*choro choro*]：少量の水が流れる時の音やその状態。小さな動物が動き回る様子も表す。
The sound or state of a thin flow of water. It also describes the condition of a small animal moving around.

キーン [*kiin*]：感覚がなくなりそうになるくらい冷たい状態。
Describes the condition of being cold almost to the point of senselessness.

カキンコキン [*kakin kokin*]：非常に固い状態を表す。「カチカチ」や「カチンカチン」「カチンコチン」も使われる。
Describes the state of being firmly solid. The terms *kachi kachi*, *kachin kachin* and *kachin kochin* are also used.

サラサラ [*sara sara*]：よどみない水の流れを表す。
Describes smoothly flowing water.

Seasons & Nature

秋の音

① **harat／hira hira**
② **saku saku**
③ **shiin**
　— *Kanshoteki na shizukesa ga **shimijimi** tsutawattekuru aki ga daisuki!*（I love autumn, when tranquil melancholy fills my heart.）

解説

ハラッ［*harat*］：小さく軽い物が解き放たれた時の音（類：パラッ）。
　A sound made when a small, light object is released. Its synonym is *parat*.

ヒラヒラ［*hira hira*］：小さくて薄く軽い物が舞い落ちる時の音。そのような物が揺れている時の音も表す。
　The sound made when something small, thin and light appears to dance in the air while falling. It also means the sound made when the object is shaking.

サクサク［*saku saku*］：薄く軽い物が粉々に砕かれる時の音。ここでは，薄く乾燥した葉が踏みつけられている音。
　The sound of a thin, dry substance being broken into pieces. In this case, the sound of thin, dry grass being stepped on.

シーン［*shiin*］：静寂な状態を表す。
　This describes a situation in which all is silent.

シミジミ［*shimijimi*］：心から深く感じるさま。
　Describes the condition of feeling heartily.

雪の日①

① **chira hora**
② **shin shin**
　― **Bota** yuki ni natta. (The snowflakes are getting big and wet.)
　gusha gusha
③ ― Koru to suberu kara chui shinakya … (Have to watch that I don't slip on the ice.)
　zuru ／ ot (to)

解説

チラホラ [*chira hora*]：小さく少量のものがあちらこちらに見える様子。
Describes a situation in which something small can be seen here and there in small portions.

シンシン [*shin shin*]：雪が降り続けるときの静けさを表す。
Describes the stillness when snow keeps falling.

ボタ [*bota*]：「ぼた雪」，あるいは「ぼたん雪」は比較的水分を多く含み，大きい粒で降り落ちる雪のこと。「ボタッ」は大きい水滴が落ちるときの鈍い音を表す。
Botayuki, or *botanyuki*, is a kind of snow that contains relatively high moisture and is falling in large flakes. *Botat* refers to the dull sound made when a large drop of water falls.

グシャグシャ [*gusha gusha*]：水分を含んでいたり，壊されたりすることで形が崩れる様子を表す。
Describes a situation in which something loses its shape because it contains moisture or gets crushed.

ズル（ッ） [*zuru(t)*]：比較的重い物を引きずったり，滑らせたりするさま。
Refers to briefly dragging or sliding something relatively heavy.

オッ [*ot*]：突然の出来事に驚いたときの声。
An exclamation made when one is surprised at a sudden event.

雪の日 ②

気温がぐんぐんさがり…

①

雪はずんずん積もる

②

でも、春がじわじわ近づいてる証しだよ…！

③

解説

グングン [*gun gun*]：変化が連続して加速度的に起きる様子。
Refers to changes occurring continuously at an accelerating pace.

ズンズン [*zun zun*]：急速に進行するさま。
Describes rapid progress.

サクサク [*saku saku*]：細かい粒子状や繊維状の物が砕かれたりする様子や音。ここでは積もった雪を踏んでいる音。
Describes the action or sound of something with a grainlike or fibrous texture being broken, torn or crunched. In this case, the term describes the sound of crushing a layer of snow.

ジワジワ [*jiwa jiwa*]：ゆっくりだが確実に進む意味合い。
Indicates slow, but steady progress.

① — *Kion ga **gun gun** sagari* ... (The temperature is getting lower and lower ...)
② — *Yuki wa **zun zun** tsumoru.* (The snow is building up more and more ...)
saku saku
③ — *Demo, haru ga **jiwa jiwa** chikazuiteru akashi da yo ...!* (But it's also a sign that spring is gradually on its way.)

コケコッコオ

日本語50音順索引

ア

アクセク	109
アタフタ	13, 163
アツ	163
アツアツ	58
アッサリ	65
アッハッハッ	81
アップアップ	143
アハハ	81

イ

イッヒッヒ	81
イヒヒ	81
イライラ	11, 29, 91, 98, 110, 141

ウ

ウェーン	82
ウキウキ	96, 119
ウジウジ	90
ウッ	75
ウッフッフッ	81
ウトウト	39, 108
ウフフ	81
ウロウロ	33
ウワァッ（ウワーッ）	30

エ

エッヘッヘッ	81
エヘヘ	81

オ

オギャー　オギャー	82
オッ	177
オッチョコチョイ	132
オッホッホ	81
オホホ	81
オロオロ	33

カ

カーッ	127, 157
ガーン	135
カキンコキン	175
ガクッ	28, 30, 110
ガクン	143
カサカサ	152
ガサガサ	70
ガサゴソ	87
カシャ	47
ガタ	23, 116
カタカタ	146
ガタガタ	40, 152
ガツガツ	10, 55, 70
カッカッカ	80
ガックリ	84, 90, 120
ガッチリ	120
カツン	28
ガブッ	64
カポ	116
ガミガミ	83, 86, 99
ガヤガヤ	13
カラカラ	161
カラッ	172
カリカリ	99
ガリガリ	112
カンカン	22, 94, 157, 161
ガンガン	138

キ

キーン	75, 175
キキキ	80
キコキコ	34
ギコギコ	22
キシキシ	122
ギシギシ	23
ギトギト	65
ギュウ	74
ギュウギュウ	142
ギューッ	51
キュッキュッ	154
ギュッギュッ	128
キュン	92
キョトン	39, 93, 150
キョロキョロ	33, 98
キラキラ	117, 169
キリキリ	105
ギリギリ	15
キリッ	71
キリリ	24, 95
キンキン	86
ギンギン	118

ク

グイグイ	30, 76
グイッ	43, 71
グウグウ	8
グオオオオ（グオーッ）	163
ククク	80
ククッ	140
グサッ	140
グシャグシャ	177
グシュ	84, 92
グショグショ	150
クタクタ	45
グツグツ	54, 56, 57, 66
グッスリ	57
クドクド	83
グビグビ	76
グビッ	144
グラグラ	46, 48, 114
クリクリ	109
クルッ	11
クンクン	63, 64, 70

グングン	138, 178	ザワザワ	45, 173	シンシン	177
				シンミリ	162

ケ

ケタケタ	80
ゲタゲタ	80
ゲラゲラ	80

シ

シイイン，シィーン(シーン)	13, 133, 170, 176
シーッ	132
シクシク	82, 114
シコシコ	62, 69
ジッ(ジィ)	32, 34, 47, 70, 103, 111
シッカリ	21, 43
ジックリ	60, 66
シットリ	61
シトシト	34, 150, 162
ジトジト	19, 157
シナシナ	74
シバシバ	111
シミジミ	176
ジメジメ	157
ジャーッ(ジャアー)	66, 77
ジャーン	87
シャキシャキ	62
シャキッ	42, 151
シャリシャリ	164
シャン	106
ジューッ	77
シュルッ	68
シュン	85
ジョキジョキ	126
ショボショボ	40, 145, 162
ショリショリ	75
シラー	88
ジリジリ	99, 141
ジロッ	32, 89
ジワーッ	68
シワクチャ	142
シワシワ	116
ジワジワ	113, 141, 148, 156, 178

コ

ゴクゴク	55, 71
ゴクッ	60, 145, 157, 169
ゴクンゴクン	71
コソコソ	133
コックリコックリ	39, 108
コツコツ	22
コテコテ	83
コホン	107
コリコリ	62, 145
コロコロ	10, 49
ゴロゴロ	8, 38, 46, 105
ゴロン	8, 108
コンコン	175

サ

サァァァ，サアーッ(サーッ)	14, 159
ザアァァァ，ザアアー(ザーッ)	159, 160, 165
サクサク	54, 56, 61, 66, 75, 153, 176, 178
サクッ	74
ザクッ	153, 154
ザザザ	26, 134
サッ	19, 44, 56, 66, 77
サッサ	151
サッパリ	19, 121, 126
ザバッ	173
サラサラ	21, 58, 170, 172, 175
ザラザラ	117
サラッ	122, 152

ス

スイーツ	49
スイスイ	12, 34, 41
スーッ	37, 140
スカーン	29, 158, 169
スカッ	29, 119, 126, 134, 144, 172
ズキズキ	102
スクスク	109
スケスケ	116
ズケズケ	140
スゴスゴ	94
ズズズ	46, 55, 58
スタスタ	34, 132, 151
スッキリ	126, 134
ズッシリ	16, 24
スパスパ	139
スパッ	54
ズバッ	90
スベスベ	117
スポッ	29
ズボッ	154
スヤスヤ	9, 57
スラスラ	20, 137, 147
ズル(ッ)	69, 128, 135, 164, 177
スルスル	69
スルッ	50, 125
スレスレ	15
ズンズン	178

セ

セカセカ	45, 46, 163

ソ

ソヨー	121
ゾリゾリ	118, 119, 124

ソロソロ	156
ゾロゾロ	37, 45
ソワソワ	98, 141

タ

タタタッ	44
ダッ	139
タップリ	26, 60
ダブダブ	123, 125
タラー(ッ)	64
ダラーン	42
タラタラ	151
ダラダラ	151

チ

チクチク	102, 105
チビリチビリ	76
チマチマ	36
チャカチャカ	137, 147
チャポッ	170
チャラチャラ	118
チャン	47
チョキチョキ	126
チョコン	47
チョッピリ	77
チョロチョロ	26, 28, 175
チョン	28, 146
チョンチョン	12
チラホラ	153, 177
チリチリ	161
チン(する)	56

ツ

ツー(ッ)	12
ツヤツヤ	116
ツルッ	55
ツルツル	65, 69, 117, 127
ツンツン	127

テ

デン	135

ト

ドカッ	25, 134
ドカン	28
ドキドキ	44, 87, 92, 93
ドサ(ッ)	9, 77, 90, 134, 153
ドスン	35
ドタ	84
ドタドタ	139
ドッサリ	25
トット	155
ドップリ	26
ドテ(ッ)	43, 136
ドドッ	155
ドドドド	173
ドドド/ドバア	171
ドバアア、ドバアアーッ(ドバーッ) 14, 151	
トボトボ	120
トホホ	23, 120, 142
トローッ	68, 122
トロトロ	60, 66
トントン	22, 54, 148
ドンドン	50, 95, 138
トントン	54
ドンヨリ	88, 165

ニ

ニコニコ	93
ニャー(オ)	8
ニューッ	51
ニョキニョキ	168

ヌ

ヌクヌク	113
ヌッ	46

ネ

ネチネチ	83

ノ

ノコノコ	42
ノビノビ	109
ノホホン	89
ノロノロ	11

ハ

バァー	93
バァーッ	88
ハアハア	43
バキッ	61
バキッ	23
パクパク	46, 72
バサッ	54, 134, 153
バサバサ	122
パシャ	26
パシャパシャ	150
バタバタ	143
バタバタ	8
パタン	146
パチッ	27
パチパチ	111
ハッ	39
パッ	99, 107
ハックショーン	104
バッサリ	126, 136
バッチリ	73, 120, 147
ハハハ	106, 116
ハラッ	176
ハラハラ	15, 92, 93
パラパラ	16, 165, 173
バリッ	61
パリッ	73
バリバリ	95, 137
パリパリ	74

バンバン	95
パンパン	125, 142

ヒ

ピカ(ッ)	8, 127
ピカピカ	17
ビクッ	39
ビクビク	33, 46
ピクピク	169
ビシャビシャ	164
ピシャピシャ	164
ヒソヒソ	18, 133
ピタ(ッ)	14, 103, 160
ヒタヒタ	44, 92, 135, 159
ピチャピチャ	162, 173
ピッ	99, 129
ピッタリ	61, 123
ピッチピチ (ピチピチ)	125
ヒヤヒヤ	15, 93
ヒュウウウ	173
ヒュルルル	163
ビュン	29
ビュンビュン	138
ヒョイ	11, 35, 72
ヒョイヒョイ	37, 41
ヒョッコリ	27
ヒョロヒョロ	21
ピョン	170
ピョンピョン	41
ヒラヒラ	41, 50, 176
ピリッ	61
ヒリヒリ	107, 124
ビリビリ	97
ピリピリ	89
ピン	135
ピンピン	106
ピンポーン (ピンポン)	25

フ

ブイ	152
フーフー	58
プーン	73
フカフカ	9
ブカブカ	128
プカプカ	139
ブクブク	10, 123
フサフサ	116
プチッ	30
フックラ	27, 168
プッツン	83
ブツブツ	18, 27, 86, 90, 97
フニャフニャ	62
ブヨブヨ	10
ブヨンブヨン	112
ブラッ	42, 96
フラフラ	36
ブラブラ	38, 88
プリプリ	86
プリン	59
ブルッ	40
フワフワ	50, 67, 174
ブンブン	29

ヘ

ペコペコ	94, 97
ペタッ	113
ベタベタ	19, 75, 152
ペタペタ	22, 124, 129
ペチャクチャ	18
ベラベラ	132
ペラペラ	16, 20, 132
ペロ	64, 75
ペロッ	70
ベロン	9

ホ

ポイ	49, 50, 63, 136
ポイポイ	87
ボーッ	102
ボーボー	121
ホカホカ	9, 57, 60, 67, 113
ポカポカ	9, 96, 155
ホクホク	67
ボサボサ	122
ボソボソ	133
ボタ	177
ポタ	111
ボタボタ	151, 160
ポタポタ	150
ボチボチ	141, 156
ホッ	13, 48, 98, 110, 136, 139, 146, 152
ポッ	60
ポッカリ	84, 174
ポックリ	84
ポツポツ	160, 165
ポツン	85
ポトポト	162
ボヤーッ	103
ホロッ	92
ポロッ	85, 114
ボロボロ	104
ポン	136
ホンノリ	168
ボンボン	86, 124
ホンワカ	9

マ

マルマル	10

ミ

ミシッ	23

ム

ムーッ	*171*
ムカァァ(ムカーッ)	*83*
ムカッ	*97*
ムカムカ	*83, 94, 102, 105*
ムクムク	*27*
ムシャクシャ	*136*
ムシャッ	*64*
ムシャムシャ	*70, 72*
ムズムズ	*104, 107*
ムチムチ	*112*
ムッ	*55, 91, 140, 152, 172*
ムックリ	*38, 43*
ムニャムニャ	*108*
ムンムン	*157*

メ

メソメソ	*82, 90*
メリッ	*23*
メロメロ	*24*

モ

モクモク	*139*
モグモグ	*56, 69, 72, 73, 74*
モゴモゴ	*90*
モタモタ	*11, 155*
モチモチ	*62*
モニャッ	*61*
モリモリ	*56, 73, 95, 144*

ヤ

ヤレヤレ	*48*

ユ

ユサユサ	*48*
ユラユラ	*48*

ヨ

ヨタヨタ	*36, 43, 106*
ヨチヨチ	*36*
ヨボヨボ	*106*
ヨレヨレ	*10, 106*
ヨロヨロ	*36*

ワ

ワーッ	*28*
ワアワア, ワ(ァ)ーワ(ァ)ー	*30, 99*
ワイワイ	*13, 99*
ワクワク	*87, 91, 93, 119*
ワナワナ	*40, 83, 135, 139*
ワンワン	*82*

ローマ字アルファベット順索引

A
a ha ha	81
a hha hha	81
akuseku	109
appu appu	143
assari	65
at	163
ata futa	13, 163
atsu atsu	58

B
baa	93
bacchiri	73, 120, 147
bakit	61
ban ban	95
bari bari	95, 137
barit	61
basat	54, 134, 153
bassari	126, 136
bata bata	143
bera bera	132
beron	9
beta beta	19, 75, 152
biku biku	33, 46
bikut	39
biri biri	97
bisha bisha	164
bochi bochi	141, 156
boo boo	121
boot	102
bosa bosa	122
boso boso	133
bota	177
bota bota	151, 160
boyaat	103
buka buka	128
buku buku	10, 123
bun bun	29
bura bura	38, 88
burat	42, 96
burutt	40
butsu butsu	18, 27, 86, 90, 97
buyo buyo	10
byun	29
byun byun	138

C
chaka chaka	137, 147
chan	47
chapot	170
chara chara	118
chibiri chibiri	76
chiku chiku	102, 105
chima chima	36
chin(suru)	56
chira hora	153, 177
chiri chiri	161
choki choki	126
chokon	47
chon	28, 146
chon chon	12
choppiri	77
choro choro	26, 28, 175

D
dabu dabu	123, 125
dara dara	151
daraan	42
dat	139
den	135
dobaat	14, 151
do do do do	173
do do do/dobaa	171
dodot	155
dokan	28
dokat	25, 134
doki doki	44, 87, 92, 93
don don	50, 95, 138
donyori	88, 165
doppuri	26
dosa(t)	9, 77, 90, 134, 153
dossari	25
dosun	35
dota	84
dota dota	139
dote(t)	43, 136

E
e he he	81
e hhe hhe	81

F
fuka fuka	9
fukkura	27, 168
funya funya	62
fura fura	36
fusa fusa	116
fuu fuu	58
fuwa fuwa	50, 67, 174

G
gaan	135
gabut	64
gacchiri	120

gakkuri	84, 90, 120	gutsu gutsu	54, 56, 57, 66	ira ira	11, 29, 91, 98, 110, 141	
gakun	143	guu guu	8			
gakut	28, 30, 110	gyut gyut	128	**J**		
gami gami	83, 86, 99	gyuu	74	jaaan	87	
gan gan	138	gyuu gyuu	142	jaat(jaa)	66, 77	
gari gari	112	gyuut	51	jikkuri	60, 66	
gasa gasa	70			jime jime	157	
gasa goso	87	**H**		jiri jiri	99, 141	
gata gata	40, 152	haa haa	43	jirot	32, 89	
gata	23, 116	ha ha ha	106, 116	jit(jii)	32, 34, 47, 70, 103, 111	
gatsu gatsu	10, 55, 70	hakkushoon	104	jito jito	19, 157	
gaya gaya	13	hara hara	15, 92, 93	jiwa jiwa	113, 141, 148, 156, 178	
gera gera	80	harat	176			
geta geta	80	hat	39	jiwaat	68	
giko giko	22	hira hira	41, 50, 176	joki joki	126	
gin gin	118	hiri hiri	107, 124	juut	77	
giri giri	15	hiso hiso	18, 133			
gishi gishi	23	hita hita	44, 92, 135, 159	**K**		
gito gito	65	hiya hiya	15, 93	kaat	127, 157	
goku goku	55, 71	hoka hoka	9, 57, 60, 67, 113	kakin kokin	175	
gokun gokun	71	hoku hoku	67	kan kan	22, 94, 157, 161	
gokut	60, 145, 157, 169	honnori	168	kapo	116	
goro goro	8, 38, 46, 105	honwaka	9	kara kara	161	
goron	8, 108	horot	92	karat	172	
gubi gubi	76	hot	13, 48, 98, 110, 136, 139, 146, 152	kari kari	99	
gubit	144			kasa kasa	152	
gui gui	30, 76	hyoi	11, 35, 72	kasha	47	
guit	43, 71	hyoi hyoi	37, 41	kat kat ka	80	
gun gun	138, 178	hyokkori	27	kata kata	146	
guoooo(guoot)	163	hyoro hyoro	21	katsun	28	
gura gura	46, 48, 114	hyurururu	163	keta keta	80	
gusat	140	hyuuuu	173	ki ki ki	80	
gusha gusha	177			kiin	75, 175	
gusho gusho	150	**I**		kiko kiko	34	
gushut	84, 92	i hhi hhi	81	kin kin	86	
gussuri	57	i hi hi	81	kira kira	117, 169	

kiri kiri	105	
kiriri	24, 95	
kirit	71	
kishi kishi	122	
kohon	107	
kokkuri kokkuri	39, 108	
kon kon	175	
kori kori	62, 145	
koro koro	10, 49	
koso koso	133	
kote kote	83	
kotsu kotsu	22	
ku ku ku	80	
kudo kudo	83	
kukut	140	
kun kun	63, 64, 70	
kuri kuri	109	
kurut	11	
kuta kuta	45	
kyoro kyoro	33, 98	
kyoton	39, 93, 150	
kyun	92	
kyut kyut	154	

M

maru maru	10
meri	23
mero mero	24
meso meso	82, 90
mishi	23
mochi mochi	62
mogo mogo	90
mogu mogu	56, 69, 72, 73, 74
moku moku	139
monyat	61

mori mori	56, 73, 95, 144
mota mota	11, 155
muchi muchi	112
muka muka	83, 94, 102, 105
mukaa(t)	83
mukat	97
mukkuri	38, 43
muku muku	27
mun mun	157
munya munya	108
musha musha	70, 72
mushakusya	136
mushat	64
mut	55, 91, 140, 152, 172
muut	171
muzu muzu	104, 107

N

nechi nechi	83
niko niko	93
nobi nobi	109
nohohon	89
noko noko	42
noro noro	11
nu(t)	46
nuku nuku	113
nyaa(o)	8
nyoki nyoki	168
nyuut	51

O

occhokochoi	132
o hho hho	81
o ho ho	81
ogyaa ogyaa	82
oro oro	33

ot	177

P

paaat	88
pachi pachi	111
pachit	27
paki	23
paku paku	46, 72
pan pan	125, 142
para para	16, 165, 173
pari pari	74
parit	73
pasa pasa	122
pasha	26
pasha pasha	150
pat	99, 107
pata pata	8
patan	146
pecha kucha	18
peko peko	94, 97
pera pera	16, 20, 132
pero	64, 75
perot	70
peta peta	22, 124, 129
petat	113
picchi pichi (pichi pichi) 125	
picha picha	162, 173
pika(t)	8, 127
pika pika	17
piku piku	169
pin	135
pin pin	106
pin pon	25
piri piri	89
pirit	61

pisha pisha	164	
pit	99, 129	
pita(t)	14, 103, 160	
pittari	61, 123	
poi	49, 50, 63, 136	
poi poi	87	
poka poka	9, 96, 155	
pokkari	84, 174	
pokkuri	84	
pon	136	
pon pon	86, 124	
poro poro	104	
porot	85, 114	
pot	60	
pota	111	
pota pota	150	
poto poto	162	
potsu potsu	160, 165	
potsun	85	
puchit	30	
pui	152	
puka puka	139	
puri puri	86	
purin	59	
puttsun	83	
puun	73	
puyon puyon	112	
pyon	170	
pyon pyon	41	

S

saaa(saat)	14, 159
saku saku	54, 56, 61, 66, 75, 153, 176, 178
sakut	74
sappari	19, 121, 126
sara sara	21, 58, 170, 172, 175
sarat	122, 152
sassa	151
sat	19, 44, 56, 66, 77
seka seka	45, 46, 163
shaki shaki	62
shakkit	42, 151
shan	106
shari shari	164
shiba shiba	111
shiin	13, 133, 170, 176
shiit	132
shikkari	21, 43
shiko shiko	62, 69
shiku shiku	82, 114
shimijimi	176
shin shin	177
shina shina	74
shinmiri	162
shiraa	88
shito shito	34, 150, 162
shittori	61
shiwa shiwa	116
shiwakucha	142
shobo shobo	40, 145, 162
shori shori	75
shun	85
shurut	68
soro soro	156
sowa sowa	98, 141
soyoo	121
spot	29
sube sube	117
sugo sugo	94
sui sui	12, 34, 41
suiit	49
sukaan	29, 158, 169
sukat	29, 119, 126, 134, 144, 172
suke suke	116
sukkiri	126, 134
suku suku	109
supa supa	139
supat	54
sura sura	20, 137, 147
sure sure	15
suru suru	69
surut	50, 125
suta suta	34, 132, 151
suut	37, 140
suya suya	9, 57

T

tappuri	26, 60
tara tara	151
taraa(t)	64
tatatat	44
tobo tobo	120
tohoho	23, 120, 142
ton ton	22, 54, 148
toro toro	60, 66
toroot	68, 122
totto	155
tsun tsun	127
tsuru tsuru	65, 69, 117, 127
tsurut	55
tsuu(t)	12
tsuya tsuya	116

U

u hhu hhu	81

u hu hu		81
ueen		82
uji uji		90
uki uki		96, 119
uro uro		33
ut		75
uto uto		39, 108
uwaat		30

W

waa waa		30, 99
waat		28
wai wai		13, 99
waku waku		87, 91, 93, 119
wan wan		82
wana wana		40, 83, 135, 139

Y

yare yare		48
yobo yobo		106
yochi yochi		36
yore yore		10, 106
yoro yoro		36
yota yota		36, 43, 106
yura yura		48
yusa yusa		48

Z

zaaa(zaat)		159, 160, 165
zakut		153, 154
zapat		173
zara zara		117
zawa zawa		45, 173
za za za		26, 134
zori zori		118, 119, 124
zoro zoro		37, 45
zu zu zu		46, 55, 58
zubat		90
zubot		154
zuke zuke		140
zuki zuki		102
zun zun		178
zuru(t)		69, 128, 135, 164, 177
zusshiri		16, 24

●参 考 文 献

『オノマトピア―擬音・擬態語の楽園』筧 寿雄，田守育啓編，勁草書房，1993

『英語人と日本語人のための日本語擬態語辞典』五味太郎著，ジャパンタイムズ，1989

『日本語擬態語辞典』五味太郎著，講談社，2004

『漫画で楽しむ英語擬音語辞典』改田昌直★クロイワ・カズ画，『リーダーズ英和辞典』編集部編，松田徳一郎監修，研究社，1985

『日英擬音・擬態語活用辞典』尾野秀一編著，レスリー・エマソン協力，北星堂書店，1989

『擬音語擬態語辞典』天沼寧編，東京堂出版，1974

『擬声語・擬態語慣用句辞典』白石大二郎編，東京堂出版，1982

『まちがいだらけの日本語文法』町田健著，講談社現代新書，2002

『言語人類学を学ぶ人のために』富岡伯人編，世界思想社，1996

『かがやく日本語の悪態』川崎洋著，草思社，1997

『オノマトペ擬音・擬態語をたのしむ』田守育啓著，岩波書店，2002

『現代副詞用法辞典』飛田良文・浅田秀子著，東京堂出版，1994

『現代形容詞用法辞典』飛田良文・浅田秀子著，東京堂出版，1991

『現代擬音語擬態語用法辞典』飛田良文・浅田秀子著，東京堂出版，2002

『擬音語・擬態語辞典』浅野鶴子編，金田一春彦解説，角川書店（角川小辞典12），1978

『月刊言語』2001年8月号―特集：楽しいオノマトペの世界，大修館

『擬音語擬態語使い方辞典』阿刀田稔子・星野和子著，創拓社出版，2009

みずの・りょうたろう　MIZUNO, Ryotaro

1936年（昭和11年）生まれ。漫画家。世界の漫画事情収集家としても知られる。イタリア，ブルガリア，アメリカで国際漫画賞受賞。スイス漫画美術館に作品収蔵。2018年　没。
多湖 輝『頭の体操』（光文社）のイラストや『キャプテン・フューチャー』シリーズ（全20巻・早川書房，1970〜1982年）のカバー・本文イラストを担当するなど多数の書籍に携わる。
語学関係では，日本初のフランス語聴視覚教育テキスト『Regardons écoutons et parlons』（第三書房，1964）をフランス人教諭と共著で刊行。その他『フランス語がスキになる本』（三修社，1983年。入門書ではなく，学校で教えない日常会話などを紹介した読み物）や，『13ヵ国 いうたらあかんディクショナリー／言ってはいけない言葉の本』（開高健編・講談社α文庫，1997年。せっかく覚えても人前で使えない!）でフランス語を担当。

オノマトペラペラ　マンガで日本語の擬音語・擬態語
ONOMATO-PERA-PERA
An Illustrated Guide to Japanese Onomatopoeia

2014年 6 月20日初版発行
2024年 5 月10日 8 版発行

監修者	読売新聞英字新聞部
編　者	水野良太郎
発行者	金田　功
発行所	**株式会社 東京堂出版**
	〒101-0051　東京都千代田区神田神保町1-17
	電話 03-3233-3741
	https://www.tokyodoshuppan.com/
ブックデザイン	松倉　浩
DTP	株式会社明昌堂
印刷・製本	東京リスマチック株式会社

ISBN978-4-490-20868-9 C0081
Ⓒ MIZUNO Ryotaro・The Yomiuri Shimbun, 2014, Printed in Japan